The Real Universal

Empire

Dylan Saccoccio

De

Cesare

DEDICATION

To my immediate family and the families I'm descended from, and to those
who invested in this research, including my grandmother, my mother, Ric &
Deb, and you.

CONTENTS

	Acknowledgments	i
1	Truth Is The Panacea	1
2	The Celtic-Etruscan Connection	Pg 16
3	The Basque-Etruscan Connection	Pg 25
4	Sicily, Carthage, & Egypt	Pg 37
5	Early Etruscan Sites	Pg 52
6	Tarquinii, Caere, & Etruscan Archetypes at Pyrgus	Pg 64
7	Vulci, Vetulonia, & Selvans	Pg 75
8	Mythological Imperialism	Pg 83
9	Alleged Orientalism	Pg 94
10	Etruscan Rome	Pg 103
11	Volaterrae & Clusium	Pg 108
12	Veii & Murlo	Pg 116
13	Dismantling the Demaratian Narrative	Pg 125
14	Villanova, Pompeii, & European Languages	Pg 138
15	Amber & Nordic Expansion	Pg 147
16	Irish & Punic-Maltese	Pg 153
17	One Source	Pg 171

ACKNOWLEDGMENTS

Thank you to those who gave me a platform over the last year or directly funded this work through my Substack, whether you agreed or disagreed with its premise.

Chance Garton, Patrick Daly, Gabe (Slick Dissident), Crrow777, Jason Lindgren, Rose777, Shën Rustemi, Erin Summer, The Lady Palace Podcast, Rich McClellan, Alan Ericson, Conor Logan, Jennifer McLauchlen, Christopher M. Jackson, Nelson Torres, Beth Martens.

1 TRUTH IS THE PANACEA

How would you feel if you learned you were descended from a king? What about an emperor, or a mighty warrior? What if you found out you were descended from a famous explorer or inventor? Would you be comfortable with your current situation and satisfied by the mere acknowledgement of your ancestor? Or would you reflect on your life and take more action to achieve greatness and impress your ancestor? Would your ancestors take pride in the work you've done? What would it mean to you if the origins of your family, ethnicity, culture, and traditions were different than what you were taught? How would you feel if what others claimed about your family was untrue?

Do you know who you are? Are you sure? Can you name your great grandparents? Do you even know your grandmothers' maiden names? What about their mothers' maiden names? Our ancestors placed great importance on knowing oneself, and knowing the Truth. The Truth can be defined as **what is**, or **all that is**. The Truth is a result of **what was**, or **all that was**. But if you could only use one word to define **Truth**, it'd be *facts*.

Nature has its cycles, whether seasons, days, hours, or the lives of its inhabitants, be they flora or fauna. The same can be said for nations and anything created by man. This death and birth cycle is mirrored across all scales of existence, by the sun and our lives, for it is a mechanism of the creation that ensures stability through change. It is to our benefit that nothing lasts forever because it means despotism cannot last forever. No matter how bleak the night is, dawn will come. No matter how barren winter is, spring will come.

Politicians don't make a nation great. Its people do. It is the people that make a city beautiful. The way we behave and treat each other will impact our community more than anything else, so don't lose your code of honor or ethics when circumstances change.

There are always lessons to be learned, values to be added, and successes to be had, regardless of the cycle. Failure only exists if you don't try and wish you had. Making lifestyle changes starts with making mindset changes. No one owes you anything. Treat your life like a business and look for ways to improve it. ***Do not despair***. Your mindset will determine the quality of your life, regardless of the cycle you live in. It will benefit you to be aware of the climate, and help others become aware of it, because only through a shift in mass awareness will people take constructive action (without violence) to change it, so that the system returns to an impartial rule of law for the benefit of all.

Becoming your best version will benefit your family, friends, and community. Once you've helped yourself, you'll be in a position to help others. Choose victor consciousness over victim consciousness. Victims are powerless to change their circumstances. Victors take responsibility and make it happen. Perceived problems are blessings to help you overcome obstacles and level up your character. Rest assured, there will be a never-ending cycle of problems and solutions. Each set of problems solved will level you up and introduce a new set of problems to find solutions for. Discontent is important for motivation, but don't let it derail you from enjoying life with those you care about. Tomorrow isn't promised, so do what you love today, no matter what challenges lie ahead.

From the Temple of Delphi's inscription "Know Thyself" to the Biblical passage "And ye shall know the Truth, and the Truth shall make you free" (*John 8:32*), it's clear that our ancestors revered **knowledge**. Even the root word of **King** is **to know**, which is **ken**, or **knowledge**, because a king must know things to write the law. This begets the Saxon **Cyning**, a **king**, as well as the Gothic **Khaan**, also a **king**. **Khan** is cognate with **Cohen**, which is a **priest**.

An indirect obstacle we face in knowing ourselves is the amount of forgeries and lies about history that were foisted upon us by the nobility to make us think they have a divine right to rule. There is not a manuscript from the ancient world that didn't pass through the hands of the priests, who've committed forgery and revisions to suit their whims for as long as they've existed.

What do you know about the Etruscan Empire? If you're of European descent, your history is connected to them. The Etruscan languages are indigenous to Italy and their alphabets are Pelasgic, which is Phoenician. The status quo taught us that the Phoenicians came from the Orient, but language, mythology, alphabets, archaeology, and much more indicate that this is not the case. The ancient Italian languages are not Indo-European, and there is no archaeological evidence of mass migration into Italy from the north or east at the end of the 2nd or beginning of the first millennia BC. Urnfield culture spreads from the south to the north in Italy, which indicates it is of Italian origin and the Celtic-Germanic-Gaulic-Nordic use of it is a result of them being an ancient diaspora from Italy, not from Scythia, even though the status quo claimed Scythians were descended from the Pelasgians (Holy Sailors).

The status quo claimed the Etrusco-Phoenicians were from the Orient, and that they were remnants of those who fled the Trojan War, with even the Julian stock of the Caesar family being descended from Iulus, the son of Aeneas, the Trojan War hero, who was the demi-god son of Venus, a product of her affair with a mortal. *Caesar* is an ***exclusively Etruscan*** name, and ***Etruscan is not an Indo-European language***, meaning it has no affinity with Greek or any other language from the Orient.

The Etrusco-Phoenician and Roman languages have great affinity to the Celtic languages, and for those interested in what Caesar looked like, if his own family's phenotype can be relied upon, he was

Celto-Germanic in appearance, or in other words, blonde hair and blue eyes, which is what Celts are named after. ***Chalath, Chalta***, or ***Chelta*** meant ***yellow-*** or ***saffron-*** colored in Phoenician according to Aylett Sammes, and while he was ridiculed for connecting the Phoenicians to the Welsh, I'll demonstrate he was right. Calling someone Celtic would be akin to calling him blonde. It's not a race. There are many examples in European families where full-blooded siblings have different features, such as dark brown hair with brown eyes contrasted with blonde hair and blue eyes; this is especially common among Italians and Irish. The Tusculum portrait is the only bust of Gaius Julius Caesar, still in existence, that was made of him while he was alive (unless others should turn up through archaeological endeavors). Everything depicting Julius Caesar, other than that bust, is an imagination of the artist.

And how would I know the phenotype of Gaius Julius Caesar? It's my family and, on the cover of this book, you're looking at the patriarch of it who came to America. Domenico De Cesare was born in Marzano Appio during the year 1871. His mother, my 3rd great grandmother, was a Conti, a bloodline from which four Popes were produced. The Conti family was among the black nobles who derived their power from the Papacy and shunned publicity. Italians have a history of dividing factions into white and black. The black aristocrats sided with the interests of the Church because that's where their power was derived from.

I suspect the culture vultures see terms like ***black*** and ***white*** nobility, and confuse them with the American usage of those words regarding skin color, but this is not the case. The man I am descended from was blood-related to the black nobility and had blonde hair and blue eyes. If the Conti family were "black" in terms of skin color, his Caesar genetics would not have survived the mix. They are clearly not Asiatic or sub-Saharan African.

Puni signifies *purple* in Etruscan, the same as it does in the Latin *pœni*, and the Etruscans from Vetulonia were the first to trim their robes with Tyrian purple according to the Roman senator, orator, and poet Silius Italicus. The influx of sub-Saharan Africans and Arabs to the Mediterranean doesn't occur till much later, circa the 7th century AD. The megalithic masonry that most researchers call polygonal, or that the Greeks called Cyclopean, is *Pelasgian*, another name for the *Tyrrhenians* (Etruscans). See the region of the Tyrrhenian Sea for reference. The Greeks also called the Etruscans *Tyrsenians*, or *Tyrsenian Pirates*, and even allegorized them as *Thalassocrats* (Lords of the Sea) and *Telchines*.

According to the people in Mexico, those who built their megalithic temples were described in accordance with the Central European phenotype, which likely became the Northern European phenotype as the advancement of civilization enabled them to survive in harsh climates. One of the most impressive temple sites in Mexico is *Monte Alban*, which is essentially the same name as *Mount Alba* in Italy, where the Caesars are allegedly from, as well as an ancient name for Britain: *Albion*, which originates from Phoenician words that signify *high rocks* and *white*, because that's what they saw from sea when they landed in southwest Britain.

As far as accounts pertaining to ancient geography from the historical record go, Polybius wrote, "For as concerning Asia and Libya (Africa was referred to as such back then), where they join with one another about Æthiopia, no one can say perfectly, to this day, whether it be a continent running to the south, or whether it be encompassed by the sea. So likewise, *what lies between Tanais* (north of the Black Sea) *and Narbo* (Narbonne, France) *stretching northward, is unknown to us at this present* [moment], unless after diligent inquiring, we learn something of it. They that speak or write any thing of these matters are to be thought to know nothing and to lay down fables."

That's how small the "European" civilized world was back then. It spread along the coasts of the Mediterranean and the Black Sea, and eventually around the Iberian Peninsula. *Albion* was the secret treasure of the Etrusco-Phoenicians, also known as *Bratanac*, or *Country of Tin* (Britain). Everything beyond that, regarding Europe, was primitive living, if any living at all.

The Phoenicians have nothing to do with Semitic people, even under the nonsense of that construct (being descended from Shem, the fictitious character in Abrahamic fantasy stories). Look no further than the words of Archbishop Richard Trench (*On the Study of Words*), who wrote in the 19th century, "It was Eichhorn who first suggested calling a certain group of languages, which stand in a marked contradistinction to the Indo-European or Aryan Family, by the common name of *Semitic*. A word which should include all these was wanting, and this one was handy and has made its fortune; at the same time *implying*, as Semitic does, *that these are all languages spoken by races which are descended from Shem*, it is eminently calculated to *mislead*."

William Betham wrote (*Etruria Celtica*), "It has been said that this language (Phoenician) was Hebrew, or had a strong affinity to it; but the best Hebraists have tested it without success, for the results have not enlightened the world. The Celto-Etruscan has not only an affinity, but its similarity is almost universally applicable to every Phœnician and Etruscan inscription to which it has been applied."

The concept of Semitic language is less than three centuries old. Which of you, who disagree, have more authority and credentials than an Archbishop of the universal priesthood that created your education system and the mapping out of your languages? The Phoenicians are not from Africa. *Libya* was named after *thirst* by Phoenicians, it being a *desert*, not the cradle of civilization that it's presumed to be, although parts of *Africa* along the Nile were perfect for civilization. The name *Africa* is derived from Phoenician to signify its *abundance of corn* and being a granary for the world (corn pertained to grains back then, not maize).

The Etruscans, who are Pelasgians, whose alphabet is original Phoenician, are indigenous to Italy. If you study the remains of the ancient alphabets of Italy, whether they be Umbrian, Oscan, Etruscan, etc., you'll see they differ more in name than they do in form. They are not descended from Greek. Latin was a lingua franca that resulted from the cultures mixing. Rome was quasi-Etruscan, which is significant given that the name *Caesar* is *Etruscan*. There is great affinity between the Irish and Etruscans, who both called God *Aesar*, and this was corroborated by Suetonius who wrote (1st century AD), "*Æsar*, id est, reliqua pars e ***cæsaris nomine*** Etrusca lingua **Deus** vocatur." (Translated as, "**Aesar**, *which forms the remaining part of the* **name Caesar**, *is in the Etruscan language the denomination of* **God**.")

The history of the Roman Empire prior to the Common Era was likely the Etruscan Empire, which is why the "history" of Rome is legendary and mythological, and no serious person can look at it and call it history. Latin was formed as a result of the indigenous Italian cultures mixing with the rest of the world, but Egyptian Thebes (Luxor) was once a capital for this empire when they possessed Asia, according to the Greek General Conon, which explains the Egyptian mummy found there, wrapped in Etruscan (Italian) script. It explains how the so-called Paleo-Hebrew alphabet is nothing more than a derivative of the Phoenician one. It'd also explain the affinity between the Celtic, Roman, and Sanskrit. It's not coming from India, or Chaldean (Aramaic), where the oldest inscriptions date to circa 250 BC, called the *Mangulam inscriptions*. The 3rd century BC is young compared to the antiquity of the Mediterranean inscriptions.

It is my opinion that the "Phoenician alphabet" came from Italy and spread in all directions through Italian expeditions, which is why Saxon letters are merely deformed Roman ones and the basis of the Scandinavian and German runes is from the Etruscan alphabet used at Clusium. The *Negau inscriptions* that were found in northeast Slovenia, near the borders of Hungary, Austria, and Croatia, were originally thought to be proto-Runic, but anyone who can read Etruscan can read these, and eventually it was conceded that the letters were from Northern Etruria (Italy). The inscriptions included Celtic names written in Etruscan. Why? Because the indigenous Italians, such as the Etrusco-Phoenicians, were Celtic, not Asiatic or African. The central European phenotype and systems of western civilization originate in Italy.

Michael Grant wrote (*The Etruscans*), "When the oldest Etruscan inscriptions in this northern region appear in about 530 BC, they are seen to employ **the form of alphabet that prevailed at Clusium**, and by the beginning of the following century this had spread right up to Venetia in the north-east, **becoming the foundation of the Venetic, Illyrian and Raetian alphabets, and the basis, too, of German and Scandinavian runes.**"

Based on the fact that the Saxons used Roman letters, I suspect they are nothing more than a branch of people descended from Romans. The root of their name is found in **sacer**, which signifies **being set apart**. This could signify good reasons such as being **holy** and **sacred**, or bad reasons such as being **cursed** and **exiled**. The Saxons were likely descended from a stock of Romans who either departed Italy for conquest, whether at the behest of the empire or their own glory, or were cast out of Rome for their disagreements with the priesthood. The fact that they had the use of deformed Roman letters indicates they were connected to the Roman priesthood in some way.

The Britons were taught that the Italian diffusion with their culture is a result of conquest. In light of the affinity between the Irish and the Punic, which is Sicilian Phoenician, and the subsequent affinity that the Welsh, Cornish, and Armoric has with the Irish language, one could appreciate the business Rome had in Britain, which was to ensure her kings continued to pay tribute. Britain had been Italy's secret treasure for the tin-trade throughout the Bronze Age, which was controlled by the maritime empire that peopled Britain. The ancient Britons were of Italian origin. Their language proves it.

Dionysius of Halicarnassus wrote, *"Indeed, those probably come nearest to the Truth who maintain that the Etruscan nation migrated from nowhere else, but was native to the country,"* as well as, *"Myrsilius of Lesbos does not call the people Pelasgians, but Tyrrhenians* (Italians; Etruscans). *And the same people were called by the rest of the world both Tyrrhenians* (Italians; Etruscans) *and Pelasgians."*

Thomas Astle wrote (Orig. Prog. Writ.), "The Punic letters are called Tyrian, and are much the same as the Carthaginian or Sicilian; they were an early branch from the Phenician stock: to make a complete Punic, Carthaginian, or Sicilian alphabet, we must admit several pure Phenician letters. *The Pelasgi were of Phenician original."*

The Tyrrhenians, another name for Etruscans, are admittedly called Pelasgians. The Pelasgian letters are admittedly of Phoenician original. Phoenicians peopled Britain, yet everything they have pertaining to language traces back to the ancient Italians. It follows logically that the Etruscans are of Phoenician stock, or the Phoenicians are of Etruscan stock, even though both names are placeholder terms given to them by subsequent cultures. There is no evidence that they referred to themselves as such, so I call them ancient Italians on account of where their languages originate, which are alien to the rest of the world's languages and thus cannot be translated.

A few centuries ago, scholars claimed the word *Pelasgos*, or *Pelasgoi*, which are Greek words, originated from the Hebrew word *Peleg*, a character alleged to be a contemporary of Noah. This is an Abrahamic claim, but it's not something that can be demonstrated. *Peleg* looks like *plg* in Hebrew (פלג). However, *Pelasgos* (Πελασγός; singular form), the plural being *Pelasgoi* (Πελασγοί), is Greek, not Hebrew. The functions of the letters *P* and *F* are represented by the same symbol in Hebrew, called *peh* (פ), the first letter of *Peleg*. This is seen in the word *Pharaoh* (פרעה), which literally transliterates as *proe*, *proh*, *froe*, or *froh* (as opposed to transliterations where people take it upon themselves to add or change letters that don't exist in the original form of the word). The Latin rendering of *Pharaoh* is for phonetic purposes. It clearly initiates with the sound of *F*.

Hebrew was a so-called dead language, not introduced as a spoken language till the Middle Ages, which is why the point system was invented to differentiate the pronunciation of certain letters; hence the Hebrew letter פּ signifies *P* while פ signifies *F*. But this differentiation, or clarity, is a result of the point system that didn't exist in Old Synagogue Hebrew or in ancient Hebrew, which descends from Phoenician in terms of its alphabet. This confusion does not occur in Greek. Greeks used *Π* for *Pelasgos*, which is the letter *P*, not *F*. *Pelasgoi* (transliteration of the Greek plural form) is Latinized as *Pelasgi* (plural) or *Pelasgians* in English. The interchangeability of this letter *P* (π), used by the Etrusco-Phoenicians (Pelasgians) at the time, was between *P* and *B* (and *V* by the Umbrians and Oscans; their letter for *B* performs the function of *V*), not *F*. For example, *Ιωβ*, transliterated and pronounced *Job* by English speakers, is pronounced *Yove*. These ancient Mediterranean cultures had other letters to serve the function of *F*, such as the *digamma*, which was developed from the Phoenician *waw*. The letter *waw*, or *vav*, was used by the Hebrew alphabet to serve the function of *W*, *V*, and *U*, not *F*. You can see this in Etruscan spellings of *Minerva* (Latin), which look like *MENRFA*, but signify *MENRVA*, as well as in Oscan or Umbrian spellings of *Minerva*, which look like *MENRBA* in both languages.

There is no preservation of how to pronounce *Peleg* (פלג), transliterated as *plg*, which could be *flg*, and is most likely *flg* based on how *Pharaoh* (פרעה) is spelled (proe/froh) and pronounced. The Greek letter to signify the sound of *F* is *Φ*, which isn't used in *Pelasgos* or *Pelasgoi*. But *Φ* is used in Biblical Greek to spell *Peleg*, which looks like *Φάλεκ*, or *Phalek*, and begins with the sound of *F*, demonstrating that *Peleg* (פלג; plg) is pronounced like *Felek* and would never be pronounced like *Peleg* on account of the *G* not being introduced into Latin till around 230 BC, meaning, prior to this, *C* served as the function of *G*. There is no *G* in the older Phoenician or Etruscan (Pelasgian) alphabets, and since the Hebrew takes its alphabet from Phoenician and spells *Peleg* with a *gimel* (g), it betrays the word's modernity. *Peleg* has nothing to do with *Pelasgos*, Tyrrhenians (Etruscans), or the people called Pelasgians, which is pronounced with a Latin/English *P* or *B* sound, not with the Hebrew sound of *F*.

The Greeks had letters to differentiate between *F* and *P* (they were not the same letter like in Hebrew), and since the oldest Greek abecedarium turned out to be Etruscan (the Marsiliana tablet), it demonstrates the Greeks never would've used a *P* for *Pelasgos* if *F* were meant. This is fact is demonstrated by their rendering of *Peleg* as *Phalek*. Would anyone still claim that the word *Pelasgos* comes from *Felek*, which could've been interpreted as *Falag*, *Foleg*, or *Fulag*? Of course not. The claim that the etymology of *Pelasgians* came from *Peleg* was based on conjecture and ignorance. The idea of *Pelasgians* descending from *Peleg* originates from Abrahamic religious zealots and gets disseminated by those who mistook them for scholars. Let the idea be henceforth known as the *Phalek Fallacy*. B. L. Ullman wrote (Etr. Orig. Rom.), "This older alphabet is identical with that which scholars formerly thought was Greek. *The early abecedaria* (Marsiliana, Formello, Caere) *are Etruscan rather than Greek*."

There is no alphabetical system in Europe that doesn't descend from Italian culture. Thomas Astle wrote (Ib.), "The characters which they afterwards used, were adopted by them in the island (Britain), and though the writing in England from the fifth to the middle of the eleventh century is called Saxon (*the architecture in England, which preceded the Gothic, is usually called Saxon, but it is in fact Roman*), it will presently appear, that *the letters used in this island were derived from the Roman*, and *were really Roman in their origin*, and *Italian in their structure at first*, but were barbarized in their aspect by the British Romans and Roman Britons."

These details are different from what I was taught in the "education system". Learning about what's going on in the world can make you angry if you're unprepared and haven't acquired a broader perspective. Regardless of how things play out, we won't benefit from being destructive. Compare it to health. If your body is failing in health, the solution is not to destroy the parts of your body that aren't functioning properly. The solution is to provide your body with the nutrients it needs to heal, or, in urgent scenarios, surgically intervene and remove the threats. The same can be said for a civilization or culture. We will always be more productive by building a better system and abrogating the authority of the previous one. But that can only done properly if we know the Truth. Therefore, the Panacea is Truth. The Truth consists of facts, and I will do my best to present you with facts, and thus contribute to the Panacea, as well as confront erroneous information that needs to be removed.

2 THE CELTIC-ETRUSCAN CONNECTION

The letter *P* has become a prominent key to unlocking the mysteries of ancient language. Welshman Edward Lhuyd helped me grasp the significance. I never read an author who claimed the Phoenicians are ancient Italians or that the Pelasgians were Etruscans, but the author who gave me the idea was William Betham. He acknowledged the significance of Italy to the ancient maritime empire (Etr. Celt. p. 142.), "Italy was the first great colony of the Phœnicians which improved on the state of civilization derived from their Tyrian ancestors, even more than Carthage."

Betham presumed the Phoenicians were from Tyre, but this cannot be true. There is nothing in the east that resembles the Etruscan language, save for the cultures they travelled to for commerce, which adopted their alphabetical system to facilitate trade. Yet the Etruscan is Pelasgian, which is of Phoenician original. The Etrusco-Phoenicians brought this system eastward. It did not come from the Orient, despite the legend of Cadmus. Were this not the case, the Celtic people would look Asiatic, as all of their languages and religious systems are products of this ancient empire. Faber wrote (Orig. Pag. Idol. Bk. IV. ch. v. ed. 4to. p. 360.), "The religion of the Celts, as professed in Gaul and Britain, is palpably the same as that of the Hindoos and Egyptians; the same also as that of the Canaanites, the Phrygians, the Greeks, and the Romans."

How could this cultural diffusion occur? There's only one group of people capable of bringing this system to the locations where it is found. Faber resolved this (Ib. Bk. III. ch. iii.), "Conon says, that *the Phœnicians once possessed the empire of Asia*; that *they made Egyptian Thebes their capital.*"

According to scholars, the Pelasgians are of Phoenician original and were the maritime empire of the Mediterranean 232 years prior to the Phoenicians. The absence of Etruscan history, along with the fables that Roman history is embroiled in, suggests something terrible happened and history was fabricated when the priest class reckoned the new era of Christianity.

Pompeii was an important site going back to the Etrusco-Phoenician maritime empire, a critical location that a region can't afford to lose without suffering substantial economic decline and social strife. If its destruction is dated accurately, then it coincides with the fomentation of the priestly takeover of Italy's institutions by

Alexandrian mystery school adepts, and the subsequent establishment of the Church. There is not one word directing the persecution of Christians in the entire body of Roman law, and simply put, it is because Christian and Jewish fables, purported as history, did not occur. There is not one Greek writer who mentioned Moses prior to c. 270 AD. There is not one work pertaining to the gospels that was written prior to the 6th century AD, which begat forgeries like the *Dead Sea Scrolls* as the dying priest class tried to revive itself. Not one historian notices Israelites, Solomon's Temple, or anything else related to the scriptures during the time they would've been noticed. Eusebius, the father of ecclesiastical history, acknowledged that Porphyry wrote **Israel** was a Phoenician name for **Saturn** (Kronos). Those kinds of details were why Porphyry's work was committed to the flame. The only archetype you'll find pertaining to the name ***Jesus*** from the first century is the Celtic **Esus**, God of War, which is the Gothic **Odin**, who is **Aesus**, named after the Etruscan word for both **God** (Aesar) and the **sun** (Esar).

Language is the Achilles heel of the institutional deception and ignorance we face because the moment a forgery is committed, it is confined to the language of the era in which it was made. The affinity that Irish has to Punic (Sicilian Phoenician) and that the Celtic has to the Roman, and subsequently Sanskrit, is uncanny. It tells a much different story than the ones you'll find in the history books. I suspect that Irish is likely the oldest language of Britain, or the remnant that kept the closest affinity to the language spoken by the original settlers, even though, in its current form, it has greater disparity to Punic than the modern Italian language has to Latin. The other languages that diverged from that original stock took the forms of Welsh, Armoric, and Cornish, which are the languages found where the earliest Etrusco-Phoenician settlements of Southwest Britain were.

The languages of Britain are not so different from the Irish once the changing of the letters is comprehended, in terms of their words, not necessarily their structures. The divergences from each other are not as extreme as they initially appear. It may turn out that some of these languages are older than Irish, such as the Cornish, Armoric, or Welsh, but no one has demonstrated their affinity to what's left of the Punic and the Irish seems to retain more of the original Phoenician words with their meanings.

There are Welsh words that are identical to Hebrew but have different meaning. For example the Welsh have tea bread called *bara brith*, pronounced the same as the Hebrew words for *creation/formation* (bara; ברא, or *bra*) and *covenant* (berith; ברית, or *brit*). *Bara* means *bread* in Welsh and Cornish, but in Irish the word signifies *traveling, anger, palm of the hand*, or a *barrow*. Henry Rowlands demonstrated that, out of the 300 Hebrew words that paralleled European ones, more than half of those Hebrew words had affinity and resemblance with the Welsh. According to him, *there are more sounds in the Welsh that agree with the Hebrew than there are in all other languages put together.*

Rowlands thought that this affinity was from the Phoenician tin-traders who peopled Britain, but he differs from me in the presumption that Hebrew was a primitive tongue, and that Phoenicians were connected to Mosaic history. I don't think Hebrew was ever a spoken language. It was a written one for the initiated. I also don't think the Phoenicians are from the Orient. I think the term Phoenician is a placeholder term for those who were also called Etruscan, or, if not the culture, the navigators among them. Hebrew takes a later version of the Phoenician alphabet, not its early one of thirteen letters, but it scarcely has any affinity to what remains of Phoenician.

I suspect the affinity of this system to the languages that are found in North Africa and Asia is a result of the empire expanding its trade from Europe, not from the priests or cultures of India migrating to Europe, as presumed in Mosaic history. My idea may turn out to be erroneous, but if not, then it may link the Caledonians (Scottish) to the Chaldeans. **Scotland**, in addition to being called **Caledonia**, was also called **Albania** (which is the same as **Albegna**, in Etruria, Italy). I also suspect somewhere in this research will be an explanation of why the **Albanian** language is drastically different from its neighbors in the east, on account of it being descended from one of the ancient Italian languages that had no affinity to Indo-European ones.

Do you suppose that the system of Hebrew and Greek letters, having the same numerological values, something that is a useful improvement to the alphabets, would be dropped by the Latins if the Latins derived their alphabet from the Greeks? Of course not. This is one of many examples of the Latin predating the Greek, as evidenced by the concession that the earliest Greek abecedaria, which were found in Italy, were actually Etruscan, as common sense would indicate, meaning the inscriptions thought to be Ancient Greek were Etruscan.

It was noticed that the interchangeability of *P* and *B* began with the **Pelasgians**, who were called **Dioi Pelasgoi** (Holy Sailors). This is seen in the ancient Italian languages such as Umbrian and Oscan. One of the most suspicious details in the chronological record is that the accounts of the so-called Phoenicians, Carthaginians, Etruscans, etc., and their history, as well as their mythology, religious rites, and other traditions, are known mostly from the writings of so-called Roman and Greek chroniclers. I suspect this was an attempt to account for the Romans and Greeks co-existing with the Etrusco-Phoenicians to make the Roman and Greek empires appear older than they were. If this isn't the case, and the Roman and Greek history is roughly as old as claimed, then I suspect the Etrusco-Phoenician Empire is far more ancient than them, and more ancient than scholars and archaeologists dated their artifacts to be.

It is inconceivable that a superior empire, such as the Etrusco-Phoenician one, could have so few artifacts and inscriptions remaining to account for its history while its alleged contemporaries, who inherited its systems, abound with artifacts and literature. Choose any nation that has gone to war. While to the victor goes the spoils, the defeated culture doesn't cease to exist from the historical record. But this is precisely what is claimed to have happened to the Etruscans after a war with Rome. The excuses and explanations for why there aren't enough examples of literature from the Etruscan

Empire to translate their language (along with the other languages of ancient Italy) are not satisfactory, especially because Rome was quasi-Etruscan all the way up to the first century BC.

Charles Vallancey wrote (Ant. Ir. Lang. p. 45.), "It is therefore impossible to come to an exact knowledge of the Carthaginian Gods, from what is delivered of them by the Greek and Roman authors. The chief Deity of the Carthaginians was **Baal**, **Beal**, or **Bel**, the Sun, to whom they offered human sacrifices. The chief Deity of the Heathen Irish was Beal, the Sun, to whom also they offered human sacrifices. The Irish swore by the Sun, Moon, Stars, and the Wind.

"The sacrifice of beasts was at length substituted among the Carthaginians, the same custom we learn from the ancient Irish historians, prevailed in this country. The month of May is to this day named **Mi Beal teinne**, i.e., the **month of Beal's fire**; and the first day of May is called **la Beal teinne**, i.e., the **day of Beal's fire** (Beltane). These fires were lighted on the summits of hills, in honour of the Sun; many hills, in Ireland still retain the name of **Cnoc-greine**, i.e., the **hill of the Sun**; and on all these are to be seen the ruins of druidical altars. (**Areopagus** means the **Hill of Ares. Arez** was an Egyptian term for the **sun**. A derivative of **greine** is seen in **Apollo Grannus**, also signifying the **sun**.)

"On that day the druids drove all the cattle through the fires, to preserve them from disorders the ensuing year; this pagan custom is still observed in Munster and Connaught, where the meanest cottager worth a cow and a whisp of straw practises the same on the first day of May, and with the same superstitious ideas. The third day of May is also at this day named *treas la samh-ra*, or the *third day of the Sun's quarter*. On this day each bride married within the year makes up a large ball covered with gold or silver tissue, (in resemblance of the Deity) and presents it to the young unmarried men of the neighbourhood, who having previously made a circular garland of hoops, &c. (to represent the zodiac) come to the bride's house to fetch this representation of that planet. To such a pitch is this superstitious ceremony carried, I have known in the county of Waterford a *ball* to have cost a poor peasant two guineas. The old Irish name of the year is *Bealaine*, now corrupted into *Bliadhain*, i.e. the *circle of Belus*, or of the Sun."

Irish people pronounce *Beltane* like *bal-tin-uh*, which I suspect comes from the Etrusco-Phoenician *Tina*, also *Tin* or *Tinia*, one of their archetypes equivalent to the Roman *Jupiter*, thus *Lord Tina* (Bal-Tina) would be the etymology of *Beltane* if I am correct.

The history of Italy has been lost, specifically that of the Romans and their Etruscan predecessors, and as a result, the history of the rest of the world has been lost. But I suspect it can be recovered through an understanding of details that are overlooked and not taught in modern academia. I have yet to see a modern archaeologist or historian demonstrate superior knowledge of philology, astronomy, mythology, or religious symbolism. Subsequently, their interpretations of important discoveries have missed the mark and many of their claims were inaccurate.

Machiavelli explained what caused the downfall of Italy in *The Prince*, "When the Cardinal of Rouen told me that Italians understood little about warfare, I replied to him that the French understood little about stagecraft, for if they had some understanding, they would not have permitted the Church to gain so much power. Experience has shown that the power of both the Church and of Spain in Italy has been caused by France, and that her downfall has been brought about by the Church and by Spain."

Alexander Del Mar wrote (Wor. Caes. p. 284.), "Until our chronology is rectified, Roman history will have to be written over and over again, without its being able to impart to mankind any convincing lessons in either religion or politic. 'The laws relating to religious matters were kept secret by the Pontiffs that they might hold the minds of the multitude in bondage,' said Livy (VI. 1). 'Roman history has been falsified and its monuments destroyed,' said Plutarch (on the Future of the Romans). From these deliberate verdicts of antiquity there can be no appeal, except to archæology and a scientific arrangement of dates."

3 THE BASQUE-ETRUSCAN CONNECTION

British kings fashioned their history to mythology and claimed they descended from the line of Noah. This same chronological problem is inserted into Phoenician, Pelasgian, Etruscan, and Roman history. Canaanites are identified in *Genesis* as descendants of **Canaan, a son of Ham and grandson of Noah.** Canaan's root is **kana**, which, among its many meanings, is **to syncretize or to give up individual leanings in order to unite more effectively as a group,** while **kin'a** means a **bundle** or **pack.** The Hebrew word for **whirl** is **Tevél,** and it signifies the same thing as **Kosmos** and **Mundus. Tevél kana** is encoded in **Tubalcain,** or the **whirl of the cosmos,** the **motion of the stars,** which of course would be the descendants of **darkness** (Ham) and **time** reckoned by the journey of the sun (Noah).

In order to discover facts about ancient Italy, the status quo Biblical narrative must be debunked. The same tactic is employed with the rest of Europe. Once a portion of it is identified as forgery, the rest unravels. This Abrahamic version of history is also attached to the Basque people, yet their language uses ancient Italian words. According to Astle (Orig. Prog. Writ.), "The Bastuli were one of those colonies of Phenicians or Canaanites, who settled themselves, in the most early ages, in that part of Spain now called Andalusia and Grenada; they first began to settle near the Streights of Gibraltar, and their principal port was Cadiz."

Vallancey wrote (Irish Lang. pp. 64, 65) , "The Etruscan name of *Jupiter* was ***iu-primus atar***; and thus ***primus atar*** was contracted to ***p. atar***, all from the Phœnician ***priomb athair***, first father (note the correspondence to Prometheus, which, if the *P* is removed, becomes **Strength of God, God of Rome,** or **God of Strength—Rome Theos**); hence the Greek *pater*, and *pateros*; Lat. *pater*; Bisc. **aita**; Gothic **atta**; Thessal. **atta**; Persic, ***padder***, &c."

This truncation was used by cultures descended from the Etrusco-Phoenicians all the way up to the 1st century BC. Reference coins from Selinunte, Sicily with the inscriptions **Sard P Ater**, signifying **Sardus Pater,** or **First Father Sardus,** the Sardinian archetype who was claimed to be the son of Hercle, or Hercules. The coinage demonstrates the Sardinian influence on Carthage, and the likely descent of the latter from the former, as well as the influence of the Etruscans on Sardegna, Carthage, and ultimately the Basque people and Britons. The fountain from whence this system flows is Etruria.

The art from Nuraghic culture in Sardegna is almost inseparable from Etruscan art, adhering to their surreal and sometimes grotesque tastes. Their pottery is a technique called bucchero, which is Etruscan, and though found in so-called Nuraghic culture, some of them were produced in Vetulonia.

The significance of Vetulonia, which will be revisited in a later chapter, was highlighted through the account of Roman senator, orator, and poet Silius Italicus, "And *Vetulonia*, the *pride*, once, *of all Etruria*. That city gave us the *twelve bundles of rods* that go before a consul, those twelve axes with their silent menace (the fasces), she first adorned the high curule chairs with ivory, and *first trimmed official robes with Tyrian purple*; while the bronze trumpet that stirs the warriors, that too was her invention."

The root of *Phoenician*, which is *poeni* in Latin or *puni* in Etruscan, signifies *purple*. The Vetulonians were the first who trimmed official robes with Tyrian purple. This custom originated in Italy, not Lebanon. Therefore, calling a people the Purple Ones, likely signifies the nobility of the Etruscan maritime empire, and I suspect the Phoenicians were the Etruscan navigators. It looks like the Sardinians are descended from them, or, at the very least, highly diffused with their culture.

Iu-Primus Atar signifies *God the First Father*. Vallancey didn't mention the Sanskrit counterpart of *pater*, which is *pitar*, also meaning *father*, and if it comes from Etrusco-Phoenician, it is more evidence that this system originated in Italy. He observed *aita* is the Biscayer (Basque) word for *father*. This word is seen inscribed next to *Suri* on Etruscan tombs in Italy, which would make *Suri*, meaning *black* or *darkness*, Father Time, or *Father Death*, the *subterranean sun in winter* (or at night in the microcosm), just like *Lycian Apollo*, and this is signified by the *wolf*, an animal sacred to *Mars* and *Apollo*, because wolves are most active in winter, as well as at dusk and dawn, the boundaries of light and darkness, of life and death, thus this symbolism lends itself to archetypes who represent boundaries, such as Terminus, as well as psychopomps (guides of the souls) such as Anubis, Charun, Hermes, etc. This is likely the origin of the Norse *Surtr*, who also signifies *blackness* or *darkness*, and is a *god of war*. The Basque language is Spanish Phoenician. The Basque language incorporating Etruscan words is evidence of an Italian origin and diaspora, not an Asiatic or sub-Saharan African one. In addition to signifying *father*, *aita* (eye-tuh) also signifies *priest* and *author*, which is a *creator* or *maker*.

For those of you who propose that the Etruscans and ancient Italians are actually from northern Europe and not an Italian diaspora, provide a northern European inscription of *Aita* that predates the Etruscan inscriptions (allegedly from c. 4th-2nd century BC). *Aita* is the epithet of the Etruscan *Hades* (Suri), god of Hell, or the sun in winter, also *Saturn*, Father Time, the *Angel of Death*, hence the epithet of Father: *Father Suri*, or *Ceres* (the seed), or *Kronos*, or *Cyrus*, or *Jupiter*, or even *Christ*, whose name is also the root of *Krishna*, meaning *black* in Sanskrit.

Some scholars don't think the Greeks had any commerce with the

Britons because, according to Sheringham (de Orig. Angl.), cited by Sammes, of all the great islands mentioned by an ancient poet, Great Britain wasn't one of them.

Of the Seven ISLANDS Nature made,

SICILY the first place had

For Greatness, next is SARDO Height,

Then CYRNUS, next Jove's Country, CRETE,

Narrow EUBEA then, and CYPRUS, last

Of all is Little Lesbos placed.

This poem agrees with the order in which I suspect these islands were peopled by the Etrusco-Phoenicians. Britain's languages and artifacts prove it was peopled by Phoenicians, whose alphabet was Pelasgic, yet historians claimed the Pelasgians were a race of Greeks. The confusion is a result of Greek people calling Etruscans by the names Tyrrhenians *and* Pelasgians. The uncertain chronology and history was highlighted by Astle, who wrote (Ib. pp. 53, 54), "The Arcadians were ancient Greeks: they used Ionic letters, but at what time they first wrote from left to right is not known, as **their chronology is very uncertain.** The Etruscan, the Oscan, and the Samnite alphabets are derived from that of the Pelasgi; **they differ from each other more in name than in form.**"

Astle claimed that the ancient Spaniards used letters that were *nearly* Greek till their intercourse with the Romans (Ib. p. 86). But I remind you that scholars conceded they misinterpreted Etruscan as

Ancient Greek, which indicates these so-called "nearly Greek letters" were Etruscan, specifically those of the navigators, called *Phoenicians*, or the *Purple Ones*, who named Spain *Spanija* due to its *infestation of conies* (rabbits and other vermin). Punic, the Etrusco-Phoenician language from Sicily, would be younger than the languages on the mainland but less susceptible to change. This would make the Basque language a variant of Etrusco-Phoenician that did not come directly from Sicily, Sardegna, or Carthage. The Basque language appears to be a result of ancient Etrusco-Phoenican, probably that which was spoken at Cadiz, blended with post-Latin Spanish which makes its origin difficult to recognize. Spain was not civilized till the Augustan era. There are appeals to Augustus Caesar to send soldiers to Spain to exterminate the vermin in order to make the region hospitable. This is why the oldest Basque inscription only dates the 1st century BC, and why it doesn't have as much affinity to Punic as Irish has. These languages distinguish where the system split and evolved separately: the Bay of Biscay (or, in the broader sense, the Iberian Peninsula), and Britain.

Lhuyd wrote (Arch. Brit. p. 29.), "The *Cantabrians* or *Biscaneers* in Spain (Basque people), whose Language is presumed to be the Ancient Spanish; seem to have affected the Letter *R* beyond all other *Europeans*; as we find by their New Testament in the *Bodley* Library; wherein I observed that in Latin words they frequently changed the *L* and *N* into *R*."

As a brief aside, this may beget the rare interchange of *R* and *N* that's seen in the Hebrew *bar* (בר; br) and *ben* (בן; bn), both signifying *son*, which would support my suspicion that Hebrew is a British system using a Chaldean syntax. The change of *N* to *R* is present in the way the Irish pronounce *cnoc*, a *hill*, as *croc*. Vallancey claimed the Basque language had no affinity to the Irish, which he was adamant *was a Punic-Celtic compound* (Ir. Lang. p. 21.), "It has been generally thought, that the Irish language, is a compound of the Celtic, and old Spanish, or Basque; whoever will take the pains to compare either of these languages with the ancient manuscripts of the Irish, will soon be convinced, that the Irish partakes not the least of the Biscayan."

The Etruscan use of *aita*, spelled from right to left in the manner of which old languages are written, dated to 400-200 BC, predates the oldest Basque inscription by centuries. The Basque language contains remnants of Etruscan, specifically from Volaterrae, which is modern Chiusi, Italy (Tuscany). At the very least, the Basque stock was influenced by the Volaterraeans, even if they weren't descended from them. Hopefully this demystifies the enigma that the Basque people wrap themselves in. If you're familiar with philology, etymology, and ancient Italian history, the Basque people are no mystery at all. Perhaps, instead of being considered Spanish Phoenician, the Basque language will eventually be considered Spanish Etruscan.

The so-called Scythians are an admitted branch of the Pelasgians. The Pelasgians were claimed to rule the Mediterranean prior to the Phoenicians by over two centuries, yet their alphabet is of Phoenician original. They were also called Tyrrhenians. The Tyrrhenian Sea is on the west coast of Italy, exactly where you find all of these non-Indo-

European languages, from Ancient Liguria (northwestern Italy) down to Carthage and Malta. All of this indicates a diaspora from Italy, not from the region north of the Black Sea.

Since the Irish language does not appear to have affinity with the Basque language, but instead agrees with what remained of the Punic-Maltese in the 18th century, and Punic is Sicilian Phoenician, it indicates that the Irish stock of the navigators did not come from the Bay of Biscay but rather went straight to Britain from Sicily or Carthage. It doesn't mean they didn't interact with the Bay of Biscay or Cadiz, but it indicates they didn't stay in those locations long enough to adopt their dialects. Virgil wrote about Sicily once being connected to mainland Italy prior to an earthquake. (*Aeneid*, Bk. III, The Story of the Seven Years' Wandering.) There are no accounts like this about Britain in the historical record, which means whoever peopled it had to create seaworthy vessels. Doggerland is not a viable option because archaeological evidence indicates sea level lowered by over a meter since the 7th to 6th centuries BC, which made most of the ancient rivers unnavigable.

Sicily, Rome, and Carthage were intimately connected, if not descended from the same culture long ago. Pliny the Elder and Gaius Julius Solinus also mention the **Sicani** (Sicilians) were ***among the peoples of the Mount Albanus league in Old Latium***. The Sicans are mentioned in Virgil's *Aeneid* as allies of the Rutuli, Aurunci and Sacrani of this region. Aulus Gellius and Macrobius account for the Sicani, along with the Aurunci and the ***Pelasgians***, as the oldest inhabitants of Italy. It seems most scholars are of the opinion that the

Etruscans were wrongly confused with the Pelasgians, but I suggest, even though these placeholder terms may have nothing to do with each other, that the majority of academia has confused the ancient Italians with the Greeks because they interpret their findings based on the aftermath of the Greek mythological imperialism. The people referred to as the Pelasgians, Etruscans, and Phoenicians are indigenous Italians, as far as my interpretation of the archaeological record is concerned.

Tellus was an archetype in Rome as well as Carthage. With the interchangeability of *L* and *R*, it becomes *Terra*. In Irish, *Tel* and *Telliur* pertain to the *fertile earth*, which appears more ancient than the Indian *Tara* because these archetypes and civilizations, along with their inscriptions, predate the earliest inscriptions that the Indians can produce. I disagree with Vallancey about the Irish and Basque languages. While they may not have affinity in structure or pronunciation, they have symbolic affinity. In Greek, *Ouranos* is the *god of heaven*, but in Irish, *Uranus* was their *god over land and water*. Vallancey wrote (Ib. p. 60), "*Uir* in Irish is *land*, and *an* [is] *water*."

There are more things besides water that the Irish *Uranus* could preside over, including *ships* as well as *lies*, a *year*, *fire*, *oneness*, *union*, *truth*, *purity*, *swiftness* (Mercurial), *elegance* (the serpent), *silence* (Harpocrates), as well as being a *god of evil or badness*. It is curious that *Ana* is both the *mother of the Irish Gods* (think Anna Maria; Mary) as well as the *Son of God* (Jesus), in addition to a *drinking cup* (Crater; the sun moves through this portion of the sky in autumn). ***Ana***, or ***Annus*** (Latin), pertains to the ***year***. The ***year*** is ***the mother of the gods***. The gods are the wandering luminaries, stars, asterisms, and constellations, whose relationships to the year, their mother, are marked by the ***journey of their father***, the ***sun***, who is also ***Anna's son***, the offspring of the year, or the ***son of God***, who is the creator of it all. This is why ***Ceres***, or ***Keres***, and other archetypes related to this subject share the same root as ***Kronos***, who is ***Saturn***. ***Sator*** is ***to sow*** and ***soter*** is ***savior***. The Basque word for ***water*** is ***ura***, but it is suggested to have meant ***living matter*** earlier in history. This is the root for the Irish ***Uranus***, god of land and water. ***Lur*** means ***earth*** in Basque. This is essentially the Irish ***uir***, for ***land***. Without getting technical, there is enough between these languages to indicate some of their words were introduced by the same ancient source.

Vallancey, while he didn't claim ***Saturn*** to be of Irish origin, showed the combinations of Irish words that pertain to the symbolism of Saturn, the God of ***bread-corn*** (corn meaning seed in ancient times), who was represented by an ***ear of wheat*** on Punic medals. This is similar to ***Spica***, the ***ear of wheat or corn*** that Virgo holds, her scales (Libra) being the sign that Saturn exalts in. Saturn was not a name ascribed to the planet till the Common Era. Prior to the Greek ***Kronos***, ***Saturn*** was ***Faeno*** (this is an English-Latin rendering; according to Vettius Valens (second century A.D.), the Babylonians called Kronos ***Phaenon***). It is suggested to be a result of

Chaldean names for planets being brought to Egypt, not actually being of Egyptian origin. In footnote 24 from *Jean Rhys Bram's translation of Matheseos Libri VIII*, it is written, "Plato in the *Republic* (Book X) knew of five planets but not their names. In the *Timaeus* he says that **the planets have no names but should belong to the gods**. In a dialogue called *Epinomis* (the author and date of this work are in dispute, but the speculation mostly occurs circa 1st century BC), probably by one of Plato's pupils, **the planets are all named after the gods**, showing that in the generation after Plato the Greeks learned to name them Aphrodite, Zeus, etc."

The previous citation relies on *Epinomis* being written near the time of Plato, but it might not have been written till closer to the Common Era. The name and symbolism of Saturn pertain to the sun from the harvest through the winter months of the Zodiac, hence the Phoenician name of Saturn being Israel, and the twelve tribes of Israel being the twelve signs of the Zodiac, which are measured by the sun's journey through them, hence they are Israel's Tribes or Saturn's Children, whom he eats as he blots them out at different portions of the year. Vallancey wrote (Ib. p. 62), "**Sat**, in Irish, is **abundance**, and **aran** is **bread**; which compounded makes **Satharan**."

Sat/Sath is also **Set/Seth**, and so another Irish meaning for **sat** pertaining to **evil** aligns with the idea of the sun setting or going into the underworld, be it in the cycle of a day or a season, which would be nighttime or winter respectively. It is alleged that **Set** was a god of deserts, storms, disorder, violence, and foreigners in ancient Egypt.

Set was portrayed as the usurper who murdered and mutilated his own brother, Osiris. Hermits take their name for their vacationing in the deserts of Egypt; ἔρημος, literally *eremos*, pronounced *erimos*, is the Greek word for *desert*. One could see how Set, or Saturn, is the god of the Hermits, being that Set was a god of the deserts.

The words for *cultivated land* in Roman and Sanskrit have a similar phonetic value to the Irish *aran*, which is *bread*. It is also a name ascribed to locations in Ireland, Scotland, and Wales. The idea of *death* is present in *urn*, or *aran*, which is sort of a cornucopia for ashes, the dead. A cornucopia also holds the bounty of the harvest, which sustains life. The root of cornucopia, *qeren* (קרן; qrn), signifies *radiance*. *Light*, in Hebrew, omits the *A* and transliterates אור as *ur*, but the Hebrew letters that form the word are *aur*. The general motifs of these philologically similar words are life, death, and water.

It appears the culture split at several key locations after leaving the mainland of Italy prior to the Common Era: Sicily, Sardegna, Corsica, Carthage, Albania, Cadiz, Malta, the Bay of Biscay, Egypt, Asia Minor, and Britain. From there it splintered into more factions, extending down to Mauritania from Carthage and to the Baltic region from Britain, unless the Baltic influence is a result of the system coming from the Black Sea region, the so-called Scythian branch of the Pelasgians. The majority of the micro-divisions occurred after the 2nd century BC and closer to the Middle Ages as the technology to survive in harsh environments improved. Prior to that, it's apparent that these cultures descended from one source.

4 SICILY, CARTHAGE, & EGYPT

My work proves the Etruscans and other ancient Italians, whose languages aren't Indo-European, did not come from the Orient or Biblical characters. They were indigenous to Italy and, being in the middle of the Mediterranean, they became great mariners who spread their system and civilized the world.

With just a slight alteration in the identity of the Pelasgians, who were thought to be Greeks, but were actually Etruscans, then it makes sense how all of these languages were nearly the same and how the ancient Italian languages had no affinity to Indo-European, like Greek has.

They are indigenous Europeans. The diaspora comes from them, not Greece or Asia Minor. With this adjustment, there is no need to figure out how letters were introduced into Italy. The Etruscan is Pelasgian, which is Phoenician. The letters originated in Italy. According to Pliny, the Pelasgians brought the letters into Italy. The Pelasgic, not the Arcadian, were the more ancient Phoenician letters, also brought to Thessaly by the Pelasgians. This means the first letters were not Ionic Greek.

Given that Herodotus claimed Argolis was settled by Pelasgians (Etruscans), now examine the pyramid of Argolis with Etruscan polygonal masonry that the Greeks mythologized as being Cyclopean. Consider the words of Dr. Thirwall, Bishop of St. David's, "The most ancient architectural monuments of Europe, which may perhaps outlast all that have been raised in later ages, clearly appear to have been the work of their hands (the Pelasgians). *The huge structures*, remains of which are visible in many parts of Greece, in Epirus, Italy, and the western coast of Asia Minor (as well as the Americas), and *which are commonly described by the epithet of Cyclopean*, because, according to the Greek legends, the Cyclopes built the walls of Tyryus and Mycenæ, *might be with more propriety called Pelasgian*, from their real authors."

Several scholars noticed that the ancient Phoenician and Etruscan alphabets only consisted of 12-13 letters, but the Pelasgic alphabet consisted of 16 letters (Gorius, Swinton, and Astle). This would imply the early Etrusco-Phoenician alphabet is oldest, which means it originated in Italy, not the Orient. Daniel Smith claimed the Pelasgian alphabet had only twelve letters (he spelled them Awleph, Bet, Vav, Chet, Yod, Kaph, Lamed, Mem, Nun, Samech, Resh, and Tauv) in

Cuneorum Clavis (Plate. VII), published in 1875, but his Etruscan alphabet consists of 17 letters, which means it's a later version than the ones recognized by the previous scholars. Smith's Pelasgian alphabet contains letters that were not noticed in the 12- and 13-letter alphabets from Gorius, Swinton, and Astle, such as Bet, and he mislabels the Chet with a symbol reserved for Heh or Epsilon, which leads me to conclude Smith's alphabets can't be depended on, but I could be wrong.

Astle wrote (Orig. Prog. Writ. p. 53), ***"The Etruscan letters are Pelasgic, and several of the Etruscan inscriptions are written in the Pelasgic language***. The Oscan language was a dialect of the Etruscan: their characters are nearer the Ionic, or Roman, than the Etruscan. There is very little difference between the Pelasgian, the Etruscan, and the most ancient Greek letters, which are placed from right to left."

The Oscan alphabet is the 16-letter system, but if the more modern letters are removed (B because it was interchangeable with V, Ch which is equivalent to the Greek Chi, the F or Digamma because it interchanges with several letters including the V, W, Y, etc., and the H because it was an aspirate), then a 12-letter alphabet remains. But if the digamma were included instead of the V, as well as H for the aspirate, then the Oscan alphabet would consist of thirteen letters.

The Coptic is claimed by some to originate from the vulgar Egyptian while others claim it is an immediate descendant of the Greek, which gave way to the Ethiopian. The Ethiopian shares over 500 root words with Hebrew, which does not prove its antiquity but instead demonstrates its youth. If the languages are reliable, the Indian influence in Ethiopia and Egypt is modern. No historian noticed the Rosetta Stone during the era it was claimed to be created in. The three languages on the Rosetta Stone are Hieroglyphics, Coptic, and Greek, which are all of Greek origin and have nothing to do with older languages like Phoenician, Pelasgian, or Etruscan. There were no hieroglyphics on the megalithic structures when they were originally found, including the Great Pyramids. These details indicate the hieroglyphics are modern compared to the ancient alphabets.

Four significant guilds, or trades, intermingled in order for empire to expand and flourish in the ancient world: *priests*, *masons*, *navigators*, and *merchants*. There are more than that, but these stood out and every other profession was a derivative of them. The ruling class was an extension of the priesthood, the government being its proxy or representative. The priest class established the law, the religion, and the mapping out of languages, as well as the invention of the alphabets, which enabled messages to be delivered and their contents to be kept safe from the uninitiated. The priests were also the astronomers, who reckoned the year and the cycles of the cosmos so that society could know when to plant and harvest with precision, but also how to celestially navigate. The stonemasons were a faction of that priesthood who built the temples in correspondence with priestly ideas, including the cycles of the cosmos. The navigators also needed to be initiated into the priesthood for the purposes of controlling trade, dominating the seas, and establishing marts at strategic locations along the Mediterranean coasts and beyond. Many of the captains were related to the nobility in some way, or worked their way up through the ranks of this system to be worthy. The very word **knight** signifies a **promoted kinsman**. The merchants were essentially the lifeblood of the empire's commercial system, and so they would be responsible for setting up the marts once commercial locations were established. These ideas were replete in all aspects of the system for as far back as history can be viewed. Even though Etruscologists claimed there was less disparity between the ruling class and the common folk in Etruria, they still had a hierarchical system. There isn't enough evidence to demonstrate an Etruscan hierarchical way of life at this time, but there is evidence to suggest they co-existed with Romans all the way up to the 1st century BC, and Romans had hierarchical systems, including a priest class, for centuries prior to becoming an empire.

With the lack of literature and inscriptions remaining, we must focus on other opportunities. I prefer symbolism and language because they are universally used, and once identified, they are the fingerprints of this system. Narco Longo made an observation during a podcast we did titled *Uncovering Phoenicans: Traders or Traitors?* (YouTube channel: Old Word Florida). He correlated the **ankh**, an Egyptian symbol signifying **life**, with the root of **Ænglisc** (English) on account of the philological interchange between **Ank**, **Ang**, and **Anc**. This is the root of **anchor**. The connection is technically anecdotal, but the symbol of the **ankh** connects to every system of priestcraft around the world. The *hull* of the ship and the *mast* are based on the female and male generative organs respectively, also known as the *Yoni* (represented by some form of *O*) and the *Linga* (represented by some form of *I*). The horizontal hash marks represent a boundary, or terminus, between the material and spiritual, with the male component signifying the spiritual fire of God and the female component signifying the material womb of Creation. This can take many forms, such as life and death, day and night, summer and winter, good and evil, heaven and hell, creation and destruction, order and chaos, and so on.

These crosses have many names, including the *ankh*, *Chi-Rho*, *Staff of Osiris*, *Crux Ansata*, the *Cross of Tammuz* (Thomas), the *monogram of Venus*, the *solar rouelle* (Celtic), *Crux Hermis*, and more. The Phoenician city Arwad was located on an island whose name transliterates as *Aink*, or *Aynk*, which is similar to *Ankh*, the key of life or of the Nile, which might be origin of these symbols found in the Mediterranean. It is not out of the realm of possibility that the origin of this symbol is Phoenician, based on Tanit and her ansated cone symbol. The attributing of it to *life* could be a result of the goods and services brought by the navigators, which provided the stability to sustain civilization and improve the quality of life.

This is important because Venus is an archetype of the ocean, as is Mary (*mare*, the Latin word for *sea*), and is associated with Venice, the Venetians, and the Phoenicians. Mary is often depicted with Yoni symbolism. Whether it's *Marine Venus* (Thalassa) at Pompeii with her Telchines (who I suspect are Phoenicians), or the *Triumph of*

Venus, or *Aphrodite* (Foam-Sprung), and *Rhode* (Rhodian Law, the precursor to maritime law, mary-time), etc. these archetypes were significant to mariners. *Tanit* (Phoenician), *Tawaret* (Egyptian), *Astarte* (Phoenician, possibly Celtic), *Inanna* (Mesopotamian), and *Ishtar* (Assyrian) are also goddess archetypes connected to this symbolism.

Sicily is probably the most important location as a hub for the ancient maritime empire. It is situated where the Tyrrhenian, Ionian, and Mediterranean Seas merge. There are Phoenician, Etruscan, Greek, Carthaginian, and Roman influences in this location, making it one of the few places where every major empire of the ancient world can be studied. The same detail that makes Sicily great for studying the real universal empire is also the same detail that blends their systems and makes it difficult to determine where one culture ends and another begins.

According to d'Alviella (Mig. Sym. p. 180.), "In Egypt the Chrism was combined with the Key of Life through a whole series of modifications which have been found in inscriptions on the island of Philæ dating from the first Christians of Nubia, who were anxious to make the sacred sign of their new faith correspond with the principal emblem of their former religion."

The *ansated cones*, which look like pawn chess pieces and were used signify the goddess *Tanit*, appear to correspond to the *ankh*. In their rudimentary form, they are a triangle at the base with a circle at the top, affixed with a horizontal line between them. But sometimes these arms are bent, unlike the ankh. They are replete in

Carthage and Sicily. The *hand*, or *palm*, accompanying the ansated cone, found on stelai of Tanit, looks to be emulated in India by the Jains, along with the *gammadion*. Both symbols are found in the Mediterranean long before they show up in India, which indicates they are of Etrusco-Phoenician origin. The arms of the ansated cones sometimes appear in a posture that is similar to the way Inanna and Astarte are depicted.

Astarte may be of Celtic origin. *Astar* means *journey* in Irish, while *te* signifies a *person*, but also *warm*. *Astarte* may have been a symbol used by the navigators to signify a *person on a journey*, a *journey to a warm region*, or the *hot journey of the sun* that provides warmth to the earth, based on its declination. Almost everything that remains of the Etrusco-Phoenician languages can be tested with success using the Celtic languages. William Betham was correct in this regard. This cannot be done with the other so-called Semitic or Near Eastern languages and the ancient Etrusco-Phoenician ones. Without inscriptions, these archetypes may all be depictions of *Tanit*.

This symbolism is claimed to be Semitic by some scholars, but the Phoenicians aren't Semites. Neither is their language, although some claimed it to be. We are left with two options: 1) these symbols and monuments have nothing to do with the Orient or 2) these symbols and monuments weren't Phoenician. *Tanit* was written as *TNT* in Punic. The crown on her head is similar to what is seen on the Greek *Hecate Trisformis* and the Roman *Diana*.

Some think the *ansated cone* is a Phoenician interpretation of the

Sa symbol, signifying *protection* and associated with *Taweret*, who is an Egyptian archetype of the Queen of Heaven. If true, it syncretizes the system. *Tanit* and *Taweret* might be the same word, their difference being an effect of transposition. If the ansated cone were a symbol of protection, it would sync up with the Celtic etymology of *Astarte*. Her name, archetype, and symbol would signify the *protection of those on a journey*, which would be used by navigators like the Carthaginians. It may be evidence that the symbolism was used in the Etrusco-Phoenician maritime empire before the Egyptians adopted it. Evidence of this symbol's use in Egypt is scarce, while it is abundant in Carthage and Sicily. The Egyptian *Sa* looks like the **Othala rune**, which signifies **O**. It also looks like the fish symbol Christians used, accompanied by the acrostic name *Ichthys*, to signify Jesus Christ the Savior and Son of God.

The *Staff of Osiris* was called *chreserion*, which has the root of Christ (Chres) in it. This symbolism of **Christ**, **Ichthys**, the *ankh*, the *anchor*, the *fish*, which looks like a Yoni, and the *mitre*, is laid up in the root of *bishops*, who were called *pisciculi* (little fishes), and *episcopal*. It is connected to *Vishnu* taking the form of a *fish*, as well as **Dagon**, **Oannes**, the root of *Joannes* (John), as well as another name for Buddha being *Dag-Po* (*dag* is *fish* and *Po* is the radical of *Phoenician*). *Quetzalcoatl*, also known as *Kukulkan*, was depicted wearing a bishop's mitre in Mexico. *Sea* is also spelled *See* in English dating to the 16th century. Thus, the *Holy See* is also the *Holy Sea*. The mariners, astronomer-priests, merchants, and masons were united by a guild that utilized this system.

Solar deities are usually named after water because water gives life, and water is named after life, which was perceived to be given by the sun. *Ankh*, *Ink*, *Inca*, *Inga*, and *Ingots* share this root. Mining is what made the Etrusco-Phoenician Thalassocrats wealthy. The Americans used some of this symbolism and admitted they were not the builders of their temples. They did not mine iron or have the ability to smelt it yet by the time the Spaniards arrived. They were, however, experts at working with gemstones. The German word *angeln* pertains to *fishing*. What do we call *fishermen* in America? *Anglers*. Are the *Anglo-Saxons* the *Wise-Fishermen* (*sagax* in Latin means *wise*, and the *g*, *c*, *k*, *cks*, and *x* interchange), or *Holy Fishermen* (*sac* in Latin is found in words pertaining to *holy* and *sacred*)? Were they the *Fishers of Men*? This symbolism is similar the *Holy Sailors*, who peopled Britain. They were Etrusco-Phoenician mariners who had the use of letters, thus the Greeks called them *Dioi Pelasgoi*, or *Holy Wanderers by Sea*.

The ancient megalithic structures in Egypt did not have the hieroglyphs, Coptic, or other Greek-based systems inscribed on their walls, nor did they have the Oriental artwork decorating them. The Asiatic races that controlled Egypt were likely unrelated to those who built the megalithic temples. The fact that Egyptian inscriptions can be translated indicates their similarity to Greek, which demonstrates their youth. The Italian languages that dominated the Mediterranean cannot be translated because they are alien to the rest of the world.

The Phoenician inscriptions that can be translated are not from the ancient culture, but rather an oriental culture using Phoenician letters in a modern context.

Carthaginians and Berbers (Numidians) were initially descended from Sicilians, Sardinians, and Etrusco-Phoenicians, not Greeks or other people from the Near East. The influence from the Near East is the result of the culture interacting with the Near East on its way to becoming an empire. When an empire establishes trade routes to distant lands, those routes go both ways, and people flow to the centers of wealth and power.

Caduceus and Tanit symbolism are associated. It seems no matter which symbolism any nation uses, it can be found in earlier forms at Etrusco-Phoenician sites. Tanit is associated with palm trees, which were used to represent the year in Egypt, thus linking her to the year, or annus, hence the name Anna in Anna Maria and Inanna, but also to the Golgothic pineal gland of Aries, the ram, which would make her a springtime archetype like Venus. On a 3rd century AD votive stele, located at Nabeul Museum, the ram faces what looks like the eternal fire in the foreground of an altar dedicated to Tanit, whose symbol is placed between two palms. This would signify the sun in springtime. This symbolism is emulated in *The High Priestess* tarot card.

An open hand with an eye in its palm is also depicted alongside Tanit symbolism on Carthaginian stelai. (Reference stele AO 1023, Costa 93, at the Louvre). This is the early form of the **hamsa**, a symbol used from the Americas to the Near East, and beyond, all the way to India. Who could be the transmitters of this symbolism if not the Etrusco-Phoenicians? Did another maritime empire use this symbolism in the ancient world? Would anyone care to explain why Tuscaloosa Indians in Mississippi are using Phoenician symbols in their *Rattle-snake Disk* that is only dated to 1300 AD? Though 1600 years later than the Carthaginian stelai, it'd still be a revelation if American Indians were using the hamsa some two centuries before Europeans arrived. The word ***hamsa*** translates as the ***Protection*** (Sa) ***of*** or ***against Darkness*** (Ham). If you split the word literally, it is ***Ham-Sa***, or ***Darkness-Protection***. The darkness is the best protection for navigators, and the ability to navigate and make journeys at night protects them from piracy. Based on the hippocamp and Telchine symbolism among the stelai found at the Carthage Tophet site, I imagine it signified guidance and protection while navigating at night.

There is a Phoenician stele from Carthage that includes the ***Egyptian Triad***, also known as the ***winged solar disk***, which is from Egyptian Thebes, also known as Luxor. (Displayed at the Louvre. Dep. East. Ant. AO 23101; CIS 674; SM 392). According to the Conon, the Greek General, the Phoenicians made Egyptian Thebes their capital when they possessed the empire of Asia. The winged solar disk of Thebes may be a Phoenician invention, not an Egyptian one. *Liber Linteus*, the Etruscan script that initially wrapped the Zagreb mummy, was also found in Luxor. Etruscan amber pieces have the same stylistic facial appearance as figures carved on limestone stelai in Carthage. (Reference object image ID:

00999541001. British Museum.) The "Orientalism" that archaeologists refer to may be a Sicilian Phoenician artistic choice.

Etruria had immense natural advantages. Its soil and climate sustained summer and winter pastures for migrating flocks. Once forests were cleared and flood-lands drained, the region became the most fertile. According to Diodorus (V, 316), the highest crop yields ever known in antiquity were from Etruria.

Sardegna was an island of expert miners and possessed very early links to Etruria. Their art and pottery suggest they are Etrusco-Phoenicians. Bronze artifacts being made in Sardinian workshops were making their way to Etruscan ports in the ninth and eighth centuries BC, which, according to Grant, was around the same time that Sardinia's bronze working was at its climax. (*The Etruscans*, p. 14.)

The ***Albegna River*** in southern Tuscany flows into the Tyrrhenian Sea near ***Albinia***. It might've been a port town for the Etrusco-Phoenicians to get to Corsica and Sardegna. It may be linked to ***Albania*** and ***Albion***. The Phoenicians were also known for mining metals and having a monopoly on the tin-trade, which they mined in Britain. The Etruscans essentially have the same alphabet as the Phoenicians. One of the Etruscan regions that provided metals was ***Massetano*** (known by the Romans as Massa Veternensis and now Massa Marittima). Another was the region on the slopes near ***Campiglia***, which provided copper and tin, and iron was mined a little south from there. The island near Campiglia, known as Elba, was also famous for its abundance of metals, first its copper, then its iron. Signs of its production date to the 8th century BC. Aylett

Sammes wrote (Ant. Brit.), "About the declining of the **Phoenician** State, the **Græcians** began to Trade into these parts (Britain), and they, who before had only heard of the **Bratanacks**, which in the same sense they called **Cassiterides**, or the **Tynn Islands**; now learnt the way to them, and conformed themselves to the Name the **Phœnicians** had given them, calling them first the **Bretanick** Islands, afterwards **Britanes**."

I suspect the Phoenicians were the Etruscan navigators sent to remote places to look for resources, and that the purple they are named after is a result of being descended from, or employed by, the Etruscan city-state Vetulonia. Grant observed that the **Etruscans were fond of the purple dye** produced from the mollusk known as the **murex**. In the late Roman Republic, and perhaps earlier, **molluscs were cultivated at points along the coast including Mount Argentario**. (Cristofani, Etr. p. 59.)

Murex trunculus was cultivated along the Mediterranean coasts, everywhere the ancient maritime empire existed. The shellfish was not exclusive to the Near East. **Only fragments of the Greek counterparts of Phoenician fabrics with the purple dye of the murex have survived** according to G. M. A. Richter (*Greek Art*, 6th ed. 1969, p. 380). In other words, there is no physical evidence of this being a skillset or craft that originated in the eastern Mediterranean.

Campiglia was also known for its alum, which looks like crystal, not to be confused with aluminum. There is a location named after it, Lumiere (Allumiere) di Campiglia, between Campiglia and the sea, where tombs date to the early first millennium BC. Alum was sometimes used as medicine, but more as a binder in the dyeing of fabrics and shoe leather, which were Etruscan specialties.

Catena Metallifera, the valley of the River Cecina (leading up to Volaterrae), was rich in copper and iron. There were also metals in the Apuan Alps. Mount Amiata, the highest mountain in Etruria, had a lot of copper, some tin, and was rich in cinnabar (the source of mercury), as did Mount Cetona, which was a source of metals from at least the second millennium BC. The Tolfa Mountains were a great source of metals in the southernmost region of Etruria. Mining and smelting metals, and then working with them to produce other objects, are among the many disciplines that indicate cultural diffusion.

Masonry techniques are something that ought to be focused on in trying to discover diffusion between cultures in the ancient past. The secret nature of these techniques has likely caused the knowledge of ancient masonry to be lost. However, no two Greek temples and no two Egyptian or American pyramids are exactly alike. There are always variations. Therefore, do not let the differences in temples, or the materials by which they are made, dissuade suspicions of cultural diffusion if there are other similarities found at the locations. One of many challenges researchers face is that the accounts of history are seldom written by those lived it. Therefore, other disciplines must be relied upon. The greatest folly a scholar can commit is to be nescient of the ancient universal system of priestcraft, or worse, to ignore it.

5 EARLY ETRUSCAN SITES

Luni sul Mignone, or **Luni on the Mignone River**, in the Lazio region, is one of the oldest Etruscan sites remaining before consolidation of the villages and population growth stopped in the final Bronze Age, when their abandonment corresponds to the birth of the states of the early Iron Age.

There are carvings in the rock that are similar to what is seen at Petra, although much more primitive. Perhaps they were for fitting wooden structures into the grooves. The same types of carvings are found at *Parco Marturanum*, which is in the same area.

Further north is Genoa, in the Liguria region, which begins in the east at Luni. The origins of the name **Liguria** are unknown, but I'd submit to you that it was Etruscan, and the reason the Genoese

Empire had all the Etrusco-Phoenician trade routes, when Genoa was the commonwealth of Italy, was because it was descended from the same culture.

The *Marta River* flowed from Lake Bolsena. *Marta* is *Martius*, clearly showing the Phoenician *Maur*, or *Mar*, which is still used by the Italians and Irish to signify **great**, and it is the origin of the Roman *Mars*. This location was considered the sacred site of Etruscan origins, and they allegedly worshipped springs and standing waters, which might beget their association with marsh-birds and fish, since these bodies of water were navigable and abundant in both. This region also produced timber, reeds, and canes for the construction of houses and windbreaks. The large ancient cemeteries indicate the area was densely populated. (A settlement was found under the lake, which was thirty feet deeper in antiquity, R. F. Paget, *Central Italy: An Archaeological Guide* (1973), p. 144.)

There may be a connection between an Etruscan town and the name *Caesar*. Tarquinii was only the supreme Etruscan city-state for less than a century. Its southeastern neighbor Caere, also known as *Cisra* or *Chaisre*, which is modern day Cerveteri, about thirty miles northwest of Rome, surpassed it. *Cisra* or *Chaisre* is from a family name, *Ceizra* according to C. de Simone (SE, XLIV (1976), pp. 163-84). This is philologically *Caesar*, and the difference may be a result of accidental transposition.

Vetulonia gained its early wealth from metals. This region was 45 miles northwest of Vulci. There were two groups of cemeteries at Vetulonia, dated to the early first millennium BC, which contained cremation urns and pit-burials, which are shallow graves, usually oval in shape. The pit-burials may be a form of cultural diffusion between Italy and Egypt. The urns were either biconical or in the form of huts. ***They are nothing like what Greeks used***. These cemeteries indicate two distinct villages but there are no traces of them. Lake Accessa had a necropolis, which is on the outskirts of the metal-bearing zone of the Massetano. The Vetulonians mined this area for copper and then iron.

Scholars suppose this industry is what united the villages of the region, which gave way to the city-state, at least by the 7th century BC. A model pottery boar from Accessa, which may be about the same period (or a little later), resembles seventh-century bronze boats from Sardegna found at Populonia and Vetulonia. (E.S. Vetulonia, Lake Accessa. A. Talocchini, *L'età del ferro nell'Etruria marittima* (1965), pp. 16, 66.)

Populonia was next to Vetulonia on the north side. It was spelled ***Fufluna*** or ***Pupluna*** in Etruscan. It was a center for working with bronze at least from the 8th century BC according to Grant, based on the fine specimens of the art appearing in its tombs. The Etruscans of Populonia had access to the Gulf of Baratti, and from there they had access to Elba, Corsica, and beyond.

Instances of likely diffusion and transmission between cultures exist all over the world. Without inscriptions, we are left to guess at history based on available artifacts. Grant also conceded that a great deal of the Etruscan civilization was derived from the Phoenician region, but whether this was directly through their exploration or due to Greek intermediaries is disputed. (The Etr. p. 37.) "Phoenician artifacts" appeared in Etruria in the second half of the eighth century BC. Mound tombs, or tumuli, also emerged in Etruria through contacts with Sardegna, who taught the Etruscans how to equip the tomb-chambers with false domes. Yet these tumuli are seen in Britain (Newgrange) and all the way to India. Grant thought the Etruscans may have learned this style of tomb-making from Syria or Phoenicia, but didn't demonstrate anything conclusively, other than the fact that objects with "near-eastern character" were found in the tombs, such as ostrich eggs, Egyptian finger-rings, ivories, etc. Grant believed this was evidence that the artifacts were a result of Phoenician intermediaries, but I suspect the Phoenicians are the Etruscans.

The north and east coasts of Sardegna were Etruscan, or had Etruscan influence, because there was a community on the eastern side of it named ***Aesaronenses***, which is Etruscan. Tharros, located on the west coast of Sardegna, had the closest links of all with the Etruscans. Tharros faces Spain, where the gold came from, which the Etruscans lacked, so they traded their copper, tin, iron, and crops for it. Tharros had access to fisheries and salt-beds, which enabled people to preserve food. It was the wealthiest Sardinian city because its workshops, which imported gold, silver, and precious stones, were the largest in the Carthaginian west. (Grant. Ib. p. 35.)

Sea birds are sacred in Egypt, but these birds are often found near marshes, and marsh-birds were sacred to Etruscans. Quetzalcoatl is the Plumed Serpent, a symbol of the sun deity, and so Montezuma wore his feathered crown just as the Pharaohs are depicted with the falcon on their heads like a sculpture in the Cairo Museum, which is symbolic of Horus and the soul. *Soul* is phonetically *sol*, the sun.

The Plumed Serpent is critical. The Serpent King is ancient in Egypt. If dated properly, a Pharaoh of the First Dynasty, whose name is indicated by a snake glyph, was also called the Serpent King early in the 3rd millennium BC. Egyptologists pronounced his name *Jet*, but then *Waji*. The female counterpart is *Wadjet*. This is undeniable diffusion between Egypt and Mexico. There is only one culture known for advanced maritime capabilities at this time, and that would be the so-called Phoenicians, whose first great colony was Italy. There is an ancient universal system that was propagated all over the world through a maritime empire. If this is not the case, then forgeries were committed that fool researchers into arriving at that conclusion.

Long before the names Italy and Albania existed, the valley of *Albegna*, which had an important river, was a hinterland of Vulci (Etruria). Today it is spelled *Albinia*, but it is philologically identical to *Albania*. At the mouth of the Albegna is Mount Argenarius, now Argentario. Alba Longa (Castelgandolfo) was located on the shore of Lake Alba, or Albano Lake. The names of legendary Alban kings are Etruscan, such as *Capys* (Capua) and *Tarchetius*. (Grant. Ib. p. 97.) The Etruscan King *Viba* (or Vibe) is related to the Vulcentine house of the *Vibennas*, who came from Veii to visit his counterpart *Amulius* at Alba Longa. Grant believed Alba Longa had Etruscan contacts and was partly Etruscanized as a result of this relation. However, given that *Caesar* is an Etruscan name and they are allegedly from Alba Longa, it might be that Alba Longa *was* Etruscan.

Pottery proves diffusion but it does not establish anything beyond that on its own. There were ample amounts of Greek pottery found at Spina, dating from the 6th century BC to the second quarter of the 5th century BC. Spina had a treasury at Delphi, which is thought of as Greek, but Caere, another Etruscan city-state, also had a treasury at Delphi. Spina was predominantly Etruscan during the height of the influx of Greek material, but it did have a Greek quarter. (Grant, Ib. p. 108.) What do the Etruscan treasuries at Delphi indicate? Is it as simple as the Etruscans having a good commercial relationship with the Greeks, or might it indicate the remnants of an ancient Etruscan colony inherited by the Greeks, as Athens and Lemnos are claimed to be? The *Lemnos Stele* is Pelasgian, which historians have mistaken for a Greek culture, but I demonstrated they were Etruscan, and the Etruscan languages don't have affinity to the Greek ones. Therefore, the Pelasgians cannot be Greek, even though it may be that these cultures, or at least their languages and alphabetical systems, are all branches of an original stock.

Spina was at the mouth of the Po River near Venice. The term **Venetian** is philologically identical to **Phoenician**. The Venetians, like the Phoenicians, were also known as the **sea people**. More bronze-work from Vulci was found at Spina than any other northern city. It was a major location for the Etruscans to spread or maintain trade routes with their eastern Alpine counterparts, which gave it access to the Baltic supplies of amber. There were Venetians in the northern part of the Adriatic who, though their names were

Venetian, only spoke Etruscan. They did not speak the Indo-European Venetian. (Brendel, p. 256; A. J. Pfiffig, Sprach, VIII (1962), pp. 149-153.) My ideas resolve this. The "Indo-European Venetian language" is a product of cultural diffusion and is not an indicator of the historical Venetians, who are of Etrusco-Phoenician origin. Supposing that the Venetians are a young culture, rather than an indigenous one from Italy, is erroneous. My Venetian family is from Ferrara, which is where the ruins of Spina is located. Their name is Fortini. They have a Celtic phenotype that conforms to Etruscans, not to Greeks or Near Eastern cultures.

According to Herodotus (4:42-44), the Phoenicians were employed by Necos to sail around Africa. Though Herodotus didn't believe the account, he recorded it anyway, "For Libya (an archaic name for Africa) shows clearly that it is bounded by the sea, except where it borders on Asia. Necos, king of Egypt, first discovered this and made it known. When he had finished digging the canal, which leads from the Nile to the Arabian Gulf, he sent Phoenicians in ships, instructing them to sail on their return voyage past the Pillars of Heracles (Strait of Gibraltar) until they came into the northern sea and so to Egypt. So the Phoenicians set out from the Red Sea and sailed the southern sea; whenever autumn came they would put in and plant the land in whatever part of Libya they had reached, and there await the harvest; then, having gathered the crop, they sailed on, so that after two years had passed, it was in the third that they rounded the pillars of Heracles and came to Egypt. There they said (what some may believe, though I do not) that in sailing around Libya they had the sun on their right hand."

The status quo equates the Pelasgian alphabet to being of Phoenician original. Their mistake, or deception, was in not recognizing that the Etruscans were called Pelasgians. Dionysius of Halicarnassus wrote (Bk. I. Sections 23-26.), *"For the Pelasgians in a time of general scarcity in the land had vowed to offer to Jupiter, Apollo and the Cabeiri tithes of all their future increase;* but when their prayer had been answered, they set apart and offered to the gods the promised portion of all their fruits and cattle only, as if their vow had related to them alone. This is the account related by Myrsilus of Lesbos, who uses almost the same words as I do now, except that *he does not call the people Pelasgians, but Tyrrhenians,* of which I shall give the reason a little later.

"These, therefore, were *the first to migrate from Italy and wander about Greece and many parts of the barbarian world;* but after them others had the same experience, and this continued every year. For the rulers in these cities ceased not to select the first-fruits of the youth as soon as they arrived at manhood, both because they desired to render what was due to the gods and also because they feared uprisings on the part of lurking enemies. Many, also, under specious pretenses were being driven away by their enemies through hatred; *so that there were many emigrations and the Pelasgian nation was scattered over most of the earth.*

"Not only were the Pelasgians superior to many in warfare, as the result of their training in the midst of dangers while they

lived among warlike nations, but they also rose to the highest proficiency in seamanship, by reason of their living with the Tyrrhenians; and Necessity, which is quite sufficient to give daring to those in want of a livelihood, was their leader and director in every dangerous enterprise, so that *wherever they went they conquered without difficulty*. And *the same people were called by the rest of the world both Tyrrhenians and Pelasgians*, the former name being from the country out of which they had been driven and the latter in memory of their ancient origin. Concerning the Pelasgian nation these are his words: '*There is also a Chalcidian element among them, but the largest element is Pelasgian, belonging to the Tyrrhenians who once inhabited Lemnos and Athens.*'

It looks like Dionysius of Halicarnassus presumed the Pelasgians to be Greeks who were driven out of Etruria, and thus called Tyrrhenians, but the Tyrrhenian languages were not Greek, or related to any languages from the Orient. I suspect these are all terms for the ancient mariners from Italy, some from the west coast, who grew up on the Tyrrhenian Sea, thus being called Tyrrhenians, who begat the Ligurians, Sicilians, Sardinians, Corsicans, and Carthaginians, while others are from the east coast of Italy, from Venice down to Apuglia, thus being called Venetians, or Phoenicians. The *Lemnos Stele* is Etruscan, not Greek. It indicates the Etrusco-Phoenicians civilized the Greeks, not the other way around.

DH continued, "And Sophocles makes the chorus in his drama *Inachus* speak the following anapaestic verses:

'O mother-city Inachus, of ocean begot,

That sire of all waters, thou rulest with might

O'er the Argive fields and Hera's hills

And Tyrrhene Pelasgians also.'

"For the name of Tyrrhenia was then known throughout Greece, and all the western part of Italy was called by that name, the several nations of which it was composed having lost their distinctive appellations.

"The time when the calamities of the Pelasgians began was about the second generation before the Trojan War; and they continued to occur even after that war, till the nation was reduced to very inconsiderable numbers. For, with the exception of **Croton, the important city in Umbria, and any others that they had founded in the land of the Aborigines**, all the rest of the Pelasgian towns were destroyed. But **Croton long preserved its ancient form, having only recently changed both its name and in heights; it is now a Roman colony, called Corthonia**. After the Pelasgians left the country their cities were seized by the various peoples which happened to live nearest them in each case, but chiefly by the Tyrrhenians, who made themselves masters of the greatest part and the best of them. **As regards these Tyrrhenians, some declare them to be natives of Italy, but others call them foreigners.** Those who make them a native race say that **their name was given them from the forts**, which they were the first of the inhabitants of this country to build; for covered buildings enclosed by walls are called by the Tyrrhenians as well as by the Greeks **tyrseis** or **towers**. So they will have it that they received their name from this circumstance in like manner as did the Mossynoeci in Asia; for these also live in high wooden palisades resembling towers, which they call mossynes."

I suspect these forts are connected to the Nuraghic structures found in Sardegna, the Balearic Islands, and in Britain, as well as the Pelasgic masonry found in Italy and everywhere the Etruscans civilized, mislabeled as Cyclopean or polygonal; polygonal is an accurate description but it doesn't indicate *who* the architects were.

According to Grant (The Etr. pp. 113, 114.), Etruscan amphoras dating to 575-550 BC were found in a ship that wrecked off Antipolis (Antibes) on the French Riviera, and Etruscan artifacts were found at Vauvenargues (on Mont S. Victoire), as well as in considerable quantities near the mouth of the Rhône, close to Massalia, founded c. 600 BC, allegedly by Phocaeans. Etruscan artifacts were also found at the archaeological site of Saint Blaise (Bouches du Rhône), and sites as far inland as Vix (Côte d'Or, Burgundy), near the Celtic fortress of Mont Lassois, which indicates Etruscanization and supports my claim of an Italian diaspora, which is why the *Negau inscriptions* had Celtic names written in Etruscan. Vix commanded the routes of Rhône-Saône and Seine to the north and Alpine passes to the southeast. Massalia is Marseilles, which has Mars in the name, from the Phoenician **Maur**, meaning **Great**, **Prince**, or **Lord**. No one seems to know the etymology of this location, but it might be found in

Celtic because, according to Diodorus Siculus (Lib. V. cap. ii.), "Those who inhabit the inland parts beyond Massylia and about the Alps, and on this side of the Pyrenean mountains, are called Celtae."

The name *Massalia* might also be a result of those connected to the *Massylii*, or Maesulians, from the *Numidians* (Berbers), whose languages indicate they are remnants of this ancient maritime empire because they are connected to the Carthaginians, whose language was Sicilian Phoenician. As an adjective, *mas* means *excellent*, *round*, and *handsome* in Irish. *Al* is *God*, or the *sun*. The termination *-ia* signifies *the land of* or *the nation of*. The name *Massalia* could signify *Land of the Comely God*, or *God's Beautiful Country*, the same way we call beautiful land *God's Country*. Southern France fits this description. As a caveat, *Alia* is essentially *Elios* (Latinized as Helios), the *sun*. Massalia is a relevant location for setting up ports and marts on the way to Cadiz. Etruscan artifacts are found in Spain, North Africa, Germany, Belgium, Luxemburg, Gorge-Meillet (Marne), Haute Marne (Northeast France), Mercey-sur-Saône, Conliège, Tours, and more. This demonstrates the spread of the ancient universal empire, from which all European systems of government, religion, and alphabets descend, across the continent, to North Africa, and Asia Minor.

6 TARQUINII, CAERE, & ETRUSCAN ARCHETYPES AT PYRGUS

Tarquinii

There are many civilizations that built upon key locations, apparently known about by the Italians, but by whom remains a mystery. The chronological dating of Rome's foundation to the 8th century BC is sheer nonsense. Higgins claimed the first three centuries of Rome's history is astrotheological, not actual. Grant called the history of the Monarchs from Tarquinii at Rome a fraudulent chauvinistic story (The Etr. p. 133). On the following page, he claimed the form in which the story came down to us contains legendary and unacceptable details, and he suspected that it was the sort of story that was told in order to avoid the suggestion that a foreigner forcefully conquered Rome. However, he was of the opinion that the major details of Rome's Etruscan dynasty were still convincing on account of the archaeological finds, and that Rome became Etruscanized and urbanized around 616 BC, which lines up with the supposed dating of the Etruscan Empire's greatness.

There are no dwellings left to demonstrate how the Etruscans at Tarquinii lived, a characteristic shared with other Etruscan cities, likely because their homes were wooden. The stone edifices were usually temples, walls, or fortresses. There are walls remaining that indicate the location had a circumference of five miles, and the remains of a temple also exist on-site. Beyond these details, much of what we know is based on the findings from their tombs and the way they buried their dead. Think about your way of life. Could someone account for its history by visiting your town's cemetery? I should hope not! But this is what scholars have available. There is only one class of people that can afford tombs, and some of those wealthy elite tombs aren't even Etruscan people; they're wealthy merchants and nobility from other cultures. It'd be akin to interpreting the history of America by visiting a mausoleum in Beverly Hills three hundred years after the Constitution of the United States was written.

The Bocchoris tomb got its name from the imported objects from the east, one of which was a glass paste jar bearing the name of the Egyptian Pharaoh **Bocchoris**, which allegedly means **Constant is the Spirit of Re**, who ruled from about 730-715 BC, but it may be a forgery or an imitation of an Egyptian original, made at a later date by Phoenicians, according to Grant, because a similar example was found in Motya, Sicily. If they aren't imitations, then they are evidence of cultural diffusion. Why would anyone want to be buried with something glorifying a foreign king, unless the tomb belonged to a foreigner, or the king was not a foreigner? Could Bocchoris have been descended from Etruria? They've dated the tomb to c. 675 BC on account of the presumption of these artifacts coming to Etruria via Phoenicia, who channeled their imports to Etruria through the Greek Campanian markets. This isn't satisfactory. It would be easier to make sense of the artifacts by acknowledging that the Etruscans were Phoenicians, rather than jumping through all these hoops to reconcile how the Etruscans have Egyptian artifacts and how a mummy from Luxor was found wrapped in Etruscan scripts.

Tarquinian painters were the best in Etruria. The Greeks have nothing similar. Grant observed that their paintings on the walls of temples and houses have not survived and their tombs did not have any paintings till many centuries later. (Ib. p. 127.) Who else has magnificent paintings in their tombs? *Egyptians.* I suggest the ancient Italians have a stronger connection with ancient Egyptians than with the ancient Greeks. The sophistication seems to be flowing down from ancient Italians to Greeks, not the other way around, and this corroborates the claims of people like Bishop Thirwall, that the Phoenicians civilized the Greeks, and William Betham, that the first great colony of the Phoenicians was Italy. It is possible that the Trojan symbolism comes from Italy, and that Rome was Troy, and many of these great mythological cities have been in the same location of Italy, built upon by each successive empire. If the paintings are Etruscan, not Greek, then it indicates Etruscan mythology was borrowed or hijacked by the Greeks. The oldest painted grave discovered at the time Grant published his book was known as the *Tomb of the Bulls*, dated to 550-540 BC. The name comes from the depiction of a horseman being chased by a bull, but the main scene is from the Trojan War, where Achilles is waiting to ambush Troilus. This was the only known Tarquinian mythological painting. If the mythology is not Etruscan, then it must be a Greek tomb or the tomb of an Etruscan who was inspired by Greek mythology.

The paintings in Etruria are masterpieces that the Greeks didn't have, unless the Egyptians were Greeks. Would this mean that Italy was an Egyptian colony or vice versa? Despite all the artifacts, the interpretation of them has not enlightened the world regarding the origins of these civilizations. The fact that Tarquinii was urbanized by the 8th century BC indicates its ports were already thriving and sea-routes were established. Campania used the Tarquinian form of the Etruscan alphabet and Tarquinian exports were found along the coasts of the Aegean Sea, as well as in North Africa. Tarquinii is alleged to be the first Etruscan city-state to create a navy that became a sea power, but I don't know how anyone would demonstrate that claim beyond using the writings of historians who weren't there.

To be a maritime power would guarantee being part of an empire through culture or treaty, or being powerful enough that other empires would leave you alone, which is required in order to stay prosperous. The Etruscan and Phoenician alphabets are essentially the same. Their languages don't conform or give way to the Indo-European languages, but instead they have an affinity with Celtic.

Caere

The *Regolini-Galassi Tomb* may prove an opposite direction of diffusion claimed by the status quo. It was the tomb of a wealthy Etruscan family located a little over 30 miles northwest of Rome, dating to the second half of the 7th century BC. The Etruscans of Caere, also called Caeritans, accumulated massive quantities of gold from Pithecusae and Cumae because they were able to sell copper and iron. ***Their local metalworkers fashioned gold in styles that were indistinguishable from those of the Greeks.*** (Grant, Ib. p. 139, 140.) If this is true, then how many gold objects attributed to Greeks are actually Etruscan? The extensive use of granulation and embossing techniques in Etruscan gold jewelry were brought to a degree of refinement that was unsurpassed in skill by Greeks, and all other cultures, a mystery that is still unsolved. According to Grant, the manner in which the minute grains of gold were attached to the gold plate is not known and the question of how is not fully answered as was thought.

Villanovan decorative motifs were found in the *Regolini-Galassi Tomb*, including a fibula acclaimed as masterful in technique, as well as ***Phoenician metal bowls.*** There was also a mixing-bowl signed by ***Aristonothos,*** a nom de plume that means "***Aris*** [aristos, 'the best'] *son of a bastard* (non-citizen)". (Grant, Ib., pp. 140, 141.) I'm not sure why his name is transliterated like that because it is written as **Aristonophos**, but I could be wrong. The rest of the inscription is faded, but the graphics depict a naval battle that people suspect is between the Greeks and Caeritans (Etruscans).

One of the major inventions from Caere was the black bucchero pottery from the 7th century BC. This type of pottery was initially used for funerary purposes, but then incorporated into household use. (Grant, Ib. p. 141.) They were exported on an enormous scale and their style is unmistakable. Caere's version of bucchero pottery was thinner than the heavier type that was popular in northern Etruria.

One of the most incredible necropolises in Etruria, called *Banditaccia*, was also found at Caere. According to Grant, the mound tombs existed in pre-urban times, but the size and complexity of the ones at Caere were unprecedented. Virgil wrote of Aeneas at the grove of Caere, **founded by the Pelasgians** and dedicated to Silvanus (the Etruscan Selvans), receiving the divine armor of Venus because of the city's **reputation for smithing**. From the Aeneid (Bk. VIII, 585-625): "And now the horsemen had ridden from the opened gates, Aeneas, and loyal Achates, among the first: then the other princes of Troy, Pallas (Wisdom) himself travelling mid-column, notable in his cloak and engraved armour, like the Morning-Star, whom Venus loves above all the other starry fires, when, having bathed in Ocean's wave, he raises his sacred head in heaven, and melts the dark. Mothers stand fearfully on the battlements, and with their eyes follow the cloud of dust, the squadrons bright with bronze. The armed men pass through the undergrowth where the route is most direct: a shout rises, and they form column, and with the thunder of their hooves shake the broken ground. ***There's a large grove by the chilly stream of Caere***, held sacred far and wide, in ancestral reverence: the hollow hills enclose it on all sides, and surround the wood with dark fir trees. The tale is that ***the ancient Pelasgians, who once held the Latin borders, dedicated this wood and a festive day to Silvanus***, god of the fields and the herds. Not far from here, ***Tarchon and the Tyrrhenians*** were camped in a safe place, and now all their troops could be seen, from the high ground, scattered widely over the fields. Aeneas, the leader, and the young men chosen for war, arrived, and refreshed their horses and their weary bodies. Then Venus, bright goddess, came bearing gifts through the ethereal clouds: and when she saw her son from far away who had retired in secret to the valley by the cool stream, she went to him herself, unasked, and spoke these words: 'See the gifts brought to perfection by my husband's skill, as promised. You need not hesitate, my son, to quickly challenge the proud Laurentines, or fierce Turnus, to battle.' Cytherea spoke, and invited her son's embrace, and placed the shining weapons under an oak tree opposite. He cannot have enough of turning his gaze over each item, delighting in the goddess's gift and so high an honour, admiring, and turning the helmet over with hands and arms, with its fearsome crest and spouting flames, and the fateful sword, the stiff breastplate of bronze, dark-red and huge, like a bluish cloud when it's lit by the rays of the sun, and glows from afar: then the smooth greaves, of electrum and refined gold, the spear, and the shield's indescribable detail."

Blera has tombs from the 7th century BC that were cubed, similar to those of Caere in the 6th century BC, indicating they were connected. The landscape is treacherous with cliffs and gorges. It was a significant location of a road network that became the Roman *Via Clodia*. The Romans built the *Via Cassia* around 171 BC to replace the Etruscan route that passed by Blera. Orgola was just northwest of Blera, off the *Via Clodia*. It was called **Orcle** in Etruscan and is now called Norchia. Given that Etruscan leaves out vowels in the middle of its words, or implies them where none is written, **Orcle** could be **Oracle**. Northeast of Orcle was Axia (Castel d'Asso).

Caere became a sea power and seemed to be the best Etruscan city-state for interacting with the rest of the world and facilitating cultural diffusion. The majority of metals from the Etruscan mines flowed to Caere, which became a luxurious center of the Mediterranean world as a result of foreign demand for these metals, and though there is continuity found in the artifacts of Caere, from a pre-urban age to its urbanization, there is significant development once it encroached on Tolfa due to the increased wealth that became available to the governing class.

Strabo claimed that the Caeritans were the only Etruscans who were not pirates. (V, 3, 220.) However, there are accounts on vases that depict sea-battles between the Greeks and Etruscans, specifically Caeritan soldiers navigating and fighting on Caeritan ships. Caere abounded with the timber needed to build these fleets. Among the various timber supplies of Etruria, Virgil gave recognition to the pinewoods of Caere. (Aeneid, VIII, 597.)

Before we conclude on Caere, let us focus on Pyrgus. Pelasgic masonry, what lay people call polygonal masonry and what superstitious people call Cyclopean masonry, is present at this location in the form of **Etruscan defensive town walls, made of limestone and sandstone, neatly jointed**. It was a notable Etruscan town and port. Gold tablets with rare texts from Phoenician and Etruscan languages, as well terracotta pediment statues, were discovered there. These details support my suspicion of the Pelasgians, Phoenicians, and Etruscans being ancient Italians. The foundation of Pyrgus was attributed to the Pelasgians. It was located in a favorable position for the Etruscan trade routes and was a gateway to the sea and international contacts.

I suspect that the so-called Indo-European systems of priestcraft are a result of Etrusco-Phoenician (ancient Italian) conquest into Asia, not a conquest by Asians into Europe. It would indicate gods like **Surya** originate in the Mediterranean, not India.

A second sanctuary was discovered at Pyrgus in 1983. *Sacellum Beta* (530-520 BC), the most ancient structure, has a roof adorned with acroteria of busts of **Achelous**. Votive deposits of **Greek vases with Etruscan inscriptions** were among the objects found there, dedicated to **Cavatha** (similar to the Greek Kore-Persephone), also written like **Kautha** or **Cath**, and **Sur**, or **Suri** (the winter sun archetype, similar to Hades or Apollo). **Achelous**, though Latinized, is philologically the Etruscan *Achle*, which is how Etruscans spelled *Achilles*. Is it possible that the Greeks fashioned Achilles after this archetype, rather than the Etruscans borrowing it from the Greeks?

Suri, Latinized as *Soranus*, was an Etruscan, Faliscan, Capenate and Sabine god. He was worshipped on Mt. Soracte in Lazio. The area was sacred to underworld gods, such as Dis Pater. The worshippers of Apollo Soranus were called *Hirpi Sorani*, or *wolves of Soranus*, from Sabine: *hirpus*, a *wolf*. *Hirpus* might indicate a philological change between *hir* and *lu* because the Latin word for *wolf* is *lupus*. The wolf is a sacred animal to *Apollo*, who is also called *Lycean Apollo* because the Greek word for *wolf* is *lykos*. Thus, *Soranus*, *Apollo*, and *Dis Pater*, the Roman god of the soil, earth, and underworld, just like *Saturn*, the *sun in winter*, are the same archetype. The Etruscan way of writing *Apollo* was *Aplu*. Languages that use fewer letters are older. Why would Etruscans omit letters in Greek names if the Etruscans were younger? The female counterpart to this archetype was *Catha*, or *Feronia*. *Farro* means *grain*; this archetype likely corresponds to *Ceres* and her counterparts. She was called *Leucothea* in Greek, which indicates the *White Goddess*, so she also may be an archetype for the moon. Her sanctuary was located next to Suri's at Pyrgus. The root of *pyr* pertains to *fire, brightness, purity*, etc., in most Mediterranean languages. In the Etruscan language, *Sur* means *black*, while *Suri* is thought to mean *from the darkness*, which some equate with the underworld. Various scholars have proposed a link between *Suri* and the Norse demon *Surtr*, whose name also means *black*, or the *swarthy one*.

Surtr is mentioned twice in the poem *Völuspá*, where a völva divulges information to the god Odin. The völva says that, during Ragnarök, **Surtr will come from the south** with **flames**, carrying a very bright sword:

> *Surtr moves from the south*
> *With the scathe of branches*
> *There shines from his sword*
> **The sun of Gods of the Slain.**

Surtr, like all the other sun gods, comes from the south, or the winter solstice (Tropic of Capricorn). This is because the part of the world where this system originates experiences winter when the sun goes south in its declination. Which other sun god has a name that means **black** or **swarthy**? **Krishna**. That root word means **good** in Greek and is the root of **Christ**. Thus, **Krishna, Christ, Apollo, Dis Pater, Surtr, Surya** and all the other black gods trace back to the Etruscan **Suri**, which has the same phonetic value as **Cere, seed**, found in **Ceres. Suri** could be the root of **Sirius** and **Osirus**, which may indicate the Italians borrowed it from Egypt, or the Egyptians borrowed it from Italy. **Sur** and **Sir** are forms of **Tsr**, transliterated as **Tyre**, the alleged capital of Phoenicia. This root is also in the Norse **Tyr** and **Thor**.

7 VULCI, VETULONIA, & SELVANS

Vulci

Pliny wrote that the *Vulcentines were synonymous with Etruscans* (NH, III, 5, 52), "Volcentani cognomine Etrusci."

Geological evidence indicates the River Fiora was deeper long ago, like many other Etruscan rivers; hence the reason Vulci was founded near it. Though Vulci looks to be named after Vulcan, the Etrurian archetype for this deity was **Sethlans**, and the Etruscan word for Vulci was **Velchi** or **Velx**. However, the name is not so important as the idea of working with fire and a forge.

Vulci was north of Tarquinii. The only record of this city is in the catalogues of geographers. Not one Greek or Roman writer accounts for it. This is staggering given that it was a location of immense wealth, jewelry, metalwork, pottery, and other ancient artifacts that were discovered in Vulci's cemeteries since the 1820s. (Grant, The Etr. p. 160.) If the artifacts are legitimate, it may indicate gross errors in the chronological timeline of European history.

The *Stele of Avile Tite* is an Etruscan limestone stele, dated to c. 550 BC and discovered in two fragments. It shows a warrior in relief within a border with an inscription that is claimed to read, *I belong to Avile Tites, ...uchsie donated me.* Michael Grant mentioned that the figure's hair is a layer-wig. They are reminiscent of periwigs, worn by the aristocracy and other people of high social status, as well barristers and judges, otherwise known as templars, the portion of the clergy that specialized in judgement.

A tomb off the Fiora River has a pillar carved into stone that looks like a precursor to the Greek, Roman, and Egyptian pillars. It is called *Tomba Ildebranda nella Necropoli di Sovana, Toscana.* A tomb discovered in Vulci was named the *Isis Tomb* because its artifacts look Egyptian. The items found in the tomb allegedly date between 625 and 550 BC. The site of Vulci has not produced evidence of its evolution thus far. Instead, its evolution was found in the ruins of its cemeteries, which, even by 1856 AD, had more than fifteen thousand tombs opened.

The *François tomb* has mythology that is shared by the Greeks, but I wonder if it originated with the Etruscans. The paintings of the *François tomb* are datable between the late fourth and mid-third centuries BC. (Grant, Ib. p. 169.) They predate Roman historical writings and *represent a native Etruscan, Vulcentine tradition*. Ajax is depicted on pottery, killing a Trojan prisoner in front of Charun. Charun has blue skin. The blue skin seems overused in Indian mythology compared to Etruscan, but it looks like an example of diffusion between the cultures. I suspect Vulci is the origin of Vulcan. Charun has a hammer, just like Vulcan.

The term **Pontic Wares** is a misleading name. The pottery, which is Etruscan, has nothing to do with Pontus in Asia Minor (on the Black Sea), but the style indicates it is connected with Corinthians and Ionians, at least through diffusion. This type of pottery was found in Vulci. Pontus was an archetype of the sea. The archetype is seen in the mosaics unearthed in the Phoenician city of Lixus. The first phase of these black-figure vases was in the style of the Paris painter (c. 550-540 BC), but his real name is not known and whether he was Greek or Etruscan is not known.

No less than 40% of all Attic "black-figure" pots that were found in Etruria are from Vulci. (Grant, Ib. p. 163.) When the "red-figure" technique became predominant in the 5th century BC, the proportion rises to 50 per cent. Vulci provides the greatest wealth of evidence for the study of "Greek vases" in the ancient world, including Greece, and yet not one Greek or Roman historian mentions it. *Vulci was one of the principle artistic centers of Etruria, the main centre of Etruscan stone sculpture* (M. Moltesen, *SE*, XLVI, (1978), p. 72.), *and it became the most important center of a flourishing bronze industry in Etruria from c. 540 BC onwards* (S. Haynes, Etruscan Bronze Utensils, 2nd ed. (1974), pp. 18ff.). How could not one Greek or Roman writer notice the most important center of the bronze industry in Etruria, or the city that produced the most black-figure and red-figure pots in the world? The status quo claimed Vulci artifacts are "inspired" by their near-east neighbors. But what if they're not?

Vulcentine bronze-work was distributed around a commercial circuit directed by Sparta, with Sparta's southern Italian colony Taras (Tarentum, Taranto) serving as intermediary. (Brendel, p. 215.) Vulci bronzes (or copies indistinguishable from originals) were found in Carthage. Bronzes of Vulcentine types were found in central Europe. A fragment of a handle decorated with a frontal bearded figure, found at Heuneburg, comes from Vulci or is diffusion of its work. Sardinian objects were found in Vulci's tombs. The nobility of Europe being buried with ancient Italian artifacts indicates something more significant than cultural diffusion. It reveals remnants of the real universal empire.

Vetulonia

Vetulonia's existence is only known through literature, not historical artifacts. An archaeologist claimed to discover it in the 18th century, but there's no evidence to conclude that. There is nothing remarkable at the site to indicate the location attributed to Vetulonia is Etruscan other than an Etruscan wall. The artifacts don't have enough Etruscan script to prove that the site is as claimed. However, bucchero pottery and bronzes were found there.

The Etruscans especially revered **Nethuns** at Vetulonia. (E. Macnamara, *The Everyday Life of the Etruscans* (1973), pp. 155f.) **Nethuns** is the same archetype as Poseidon and Neptune, who, in the modern system, signify an aspect of the sun in spring, but also the sea. This supports the link between the navigators and the Etruscans, as well as their part in the ancient maritime empire. The only caveat is that the objects at the site are dated to a millennium after the peak of Vetulonia's prosperity, including the coins of Vetulonia with anchors and dolphins, as well as the monument from the time of Claudius at Caere, displaying a personified Vetulonia with a steering wheel on her shoulder (41-54 AD). They are not reliable for discovering the ancient history of this site, but the steering wheel on the coin labeled *Vetulonia Æ Semuncia*, dated to the 3rd century BC, looks like the four-spoked Gallo-Celtic solar rouelle, an emblem for the sun. This solidifies the ancient universal system of priestcraft used by the Holy Sailors.

However, the early links between Vetulonia and Sardegna solidify my suspicion of the Etrusco-Phoenicians being Celtæ who were indigenous to Italy. The false-domed tombs that came to Populonia from Sardegna c. 800 BC, which are found in Vetulonia, demonstrate this. Sardinian bronze model boats and animals were also found in Vetulonian tombs from the 7th century BC. According to Strabo (V, 2, 7, 124, 225.), Sardinian ports such as Tharros yielded many Etruscan products, which is why he called the inhabitants Tyrrhenians (Etruscans).

Finding the ports of Vetulonia is challenging because, according to Cristofani, sea level was one meter higher between 600 BC and 100 AD than it is now. Grant speculated that the higher sea level in ancient times enabled Lake Prilius to be fed by the Bruna and Ombrone rivers, or if not, canals may have linked the two rivers. (Ib. pp. 184, 185.) He claimed there was a man-made channel that augmented the deep and navigable entrances of Lake Prilius, connecting it to the sea. Traces of the buildings along the lake still exist and are dated to the 3rd and 2nd centuries BC. According to Cicero, there was an island in the middle of it in 52 BC. (In Defense of Milo, XXIV, 74.) The lagoon and its outlets to the sea are depicted in maps from the Renaissance era, but by that time it had become almost landlocked. *Casa Galera* (boat-house), *Porto a Colle* (hillside port), *Porto alle Cavalle* (mares' port), and *Piscara a Mare* (sea-fishing) are all names of the hamlets on the shores of Lake Prilius that indicate maritime activity. The English word for **female horse** is **mare**, which is the same as the Latin word for the **sea**.

Etruscan art is inspired by the world yet it is unique. The only explanation for how many influences there are in their artifacts is that they were a people of the world, a culture from Italy that became a maritime empire, reaching every port a vessel could travel to, an advantage transferred to its successors, the Romans.

Selva di Malano may be named after the Etruscan **Selvans**. There were statues of Selvans and Culsans found at the site. The Etruscan **Culsans** is **Janus**. The inscription on his leg reads, "Velia Cuinti, Arnt's (daughter) to Culsans (this object) gladly gave."

The alleged dates of these statues (300-250 BC) indicate they existed during, if not after, the days of Janus, which may be evidence that Roman history is younger than claimed. The Etruscan **Selvans** is claimed to be the Roman **Silvanus**. The Etruscans depicted him in what looks like a bearskin, but it could also be a lion skin, or a wolf skin, which would connect him to **Hercules, Apollo**, and **Mars**. If I had to guess, **Culsans** was the **winter solstice** where the year was reckoned, while **Selvans** was the **summer solstice**. Selvans is also claimed to be a **god of boundaries**, just like Terminus. Silvanus was an archetype who protected the forests and fields, as well as presided over the boundaries of properties. There were three minor versions of Silvanus called **silvani**, a trinity, and each one presided over the **home**, the **fields**, and the **boundaries**. Silvanus was a shepherd of the flocks, ensuring their fertility and protecting them from the wolves.

The Gallo-Roman version of this archetype, **Sucellus**, is depicted with a hammer and a bowl. The hammer may indicate he is a deity of metallurgy like **Vulcan, Charun**, and others related to the forge. The bowl may signify a chalice or something that wine is drunk from. If so, it'd be akin to gods of the grape. He's also similar to **Silenus**, who resembled a man of the forest with ears of a horse, and sometimes the tail and legs of the same animal. The **sileni** were drunken followers of Dionysus, a god of the grape and an archetype of the sun.

On the *Liver of Piacenza*, **Culsans** is allegedly defined as **Alpan**, which is claimed to signify **good** or **pure**. With the *P & B* interchange, we may have the root of **Albania**, or **Good Country**, or **Country of Culsans**. It's also a root in Mexican words like Tlahuiz**calpan**techutli and Zacu**alpan**, but that is anecdotal unless proven otherwise. Could **Alpan** be connected to the Greek **Apollon** or the Etruscan **Aplu**?

8 MYTHOLOGICAL IMPERIALISM

"Language is what it is." —Crrow777

Speculating on older cultures that are alleged to have existed but which yield no artifacts, such as Atlantis, is a fruitless endeavor. The Greeks had an industry of practicing mythological imperialism, where they reinvented the mythology of the Etrusco-Phoenicians, along with the history of cultures on the outskirts of the Greek world, ascribing their origins to legendary Greek founders. They did this with Etruria, as Grant noticed (The Etruscans, p. 72), in Caere, Pyrgi, Telamon, Orbetello (Cosa), Pisae, and inland locations such as Corona, despite there being no archaeological evidence of Greek origins anywhere at these locations. Even Grant conceded that *Rome was a quasi-Etruscan fringe city*. Here we have more evidence of Etruscans descending from Phoenicians and giving way to Romans, with almost nothing to do with Greeks other than what the course of commerce would induce.

I concede that the Celtic-Scandinavian phenotype is present in the Finnish and the Etrusco-Phoenician cultures, and that they are likely descendants of the same culture or region. The Etruscan word for **God** is **Aesar** (equivalent to the Latin **Deus**), which is the origin of **Kaiser**, the German word for **Emperor**. One sees this diffusion flowing from Italy, not from the north or east into Italy. This word's meaning of **emperor** or **ruler** exists in Russian (*tsar*), Czech (*císar*), Slovak (*cisár*), Slovenian (*cesar*), Hungarian (*császár*), Arabic (*qaysar*), and other languages.

Slovenian is almost one for one with the Italian version because they are ancient Italians or, if not, their country was inhabited by them. The *Negau inscriptions* found there, which were initially thought to be the oldest Germanic Runes, or a proto-Runic system, were demonstrated to be letters from Northern Etruria. If authentic, the *Negau inscriptions* may be as old as 350-300 BC. Scholars are well aware of the Runes descending from Etruscan, which is often disguised under the moniker *Old Italic*. But there is disparity between scholars and the general public because, in my experience, the general public is ignorant of this fact or they reject it in order to project a national identity that has nothing to do with Italy.

The first plausible mention of a people speaking a Uralic language is in Tacitus's *Germania* (c. 98 AD), mentioning the *Fenni* (usually interpreted as referring to the Sami) and two other possibly Uralic tribes living in the farthest reaches of Scandinavia. Tacitus's account is vague, making the location of the Fenni uncertain. He wrote, "The Venedi overrun in their predatory excursions all the woody and mountainous tracts between the Peucini and the Fenni."

This is the same as the Irish term for Phoenician: *Fenian*. Why do all the names of these tribes have derivatives of Phoenician, Venetian, or Fenian? According to *O'Reilly's Irish Dictionary*, "*Sheancus*, constitutes, both in name and matter, the original laws of Ireland, and they are sometimes called *Fenechus*, because they regulated the *Fenians* (Phœnicians) and their colonies. It was the foundation of the knowledge of the tribes of Erinn, and points out their origin, for the Erenachs (Irish) derive their name from *Fhenius Farsaid*. Phenius, the *mariner*, or *of the prow of a ship*."

The Irish-Phoenician connection is established through the affinity Irish has with Punic (Sicilian Phoenician), yet lacks with other variants of the Phoenician stock, such as the Basque language. The Celtic, the Roman, and the Sanskrit languages share so many words that they must be introduced by the same source or are the offspring from the parent. The source is likely located in the middle of the regions where these languages were used, whose artifacts are the oldest: Italy.

Kukulkan is another name for *Quetzalcoatl*. This is a Mexican archetype. It might be something they inherited from the Irish, who have *Cú Chulain*. In Mexico, Kukulkan is depicted giving the Mexicans the gift of corn. *Corn* was a word for *seed*, and it contains the symbolism of the *sun* (Kronos, qeren, cornu). Kukulkan's mitre looks Egyptian, akin to Wadjet's crown, known as the *Atef* (the feathered white crown of Osiris). If you grant me the *L* to *R* interchange (lex-rex, legal-regal, loyal-royal), *Chulainn* becomes *Churainn*, which is the Etruscan *Charun* and the Greek *Charon*.

At the Temple of the Plumed Serpent in Mexico, there is horn symbolism that's also depicted with deities such as Kronos, Jupiter, Pan, and all their corresponding archetypes. The horn (qeren) signifies both radiance and seed symbolism. That isn't the only thing they have in common. Faber observed the architecture of the pyramid in Cholula, Mexico mirrored that of the Temple of Jupiter Belus. (Class. Journ. Vol. XXI. pp. 10, 11.)

The alleged Viking wardrobe found at Newfoundland is similar to that of the Carthusian monks. According to Torquemada, the missionaries supposed that *Quetzalcoatl* was an Irishman, because he was called *Kukulkan* in Yucatan, and wore a hood and a vest covered with red crosses, and they thought he must've been a Carthusian monk, so named from the paper covering which they wore on their heads: from the Italian word *cartoccio*. Is there a *Cartoccio, Carthusian, Cú Chulainn, Kukulkan* connection with *Carthage*? This would indicate it was the Etrusco-Phoenician Britons that made it to the Americas and brought this system there.

There are significant paintings in the *Tombs of Orcus*, located in Tarquinia. A deity is depicted in the fashion of Abraxas and Serpentarius, overseeing two individuals playing a board game. One of them is named *These*, but the paint no longer exists to show the third figure's name and the scope of the scene. It looks like a high stakes game being played while *Tuchulcha* looks on (this is Abraxas, Chnoubis, or Iao). *Tuchulcha* is similar to *Kukulkan*. If the Etrusco-Phoenicians made it to America, the Etruscan archetype *Cuclu* might be the origin of the Mexican *Kukulkan*.

Ptolemy mentioned a people called the *Phinnoi* (*Φιννοι*) in his *Geographia*, written around 150 AD, who some think are the *Fenni*. He located them in two different areas: northern *Scandia* (Scandinavia), believed to be an island at the time, and a southern group dwelling to the east of the upper Vistula River (southeast Poland). But no one seems to know if these people were connected. The information is not satisfactory for making claims, but these ideas inspire some to suspect the Etruscans are from Scandinavia, or a place that is now part of modern Russia. I do not share that sentiment, but I could be wrong.

Fenni, or *Finni*, was allegedly mentioned again in the *Getica* of chronicler Jordanes in the 6th century AD. He wrote about three groups with names similar to Ptolemy's *Phinnoi*, the *Screrefennae*, *Finnaithae* and *mitissimi Finni* (softest Finns) who inhabited the island of *Scandza* (Scandinavia). The claims about the identities of these people are unclear. They exist in a time over a thousand years prior to the earliest inscriptions from the Finish people.

I'm curious as to why there are no suggestions that the reference to the *Fenni* might describe the Irish-Phoenicians. Scandia was believed to be an island. Diodorus Siculus (1st Century BC), quoting Hecatæus (6th - 5th centuries BC) and other historians, wrote about the Irish as Hyperboreans, "***Opposite to the coast of Gallia Celtica there is an island in the ocean, not smaller than Sicily***—lying to the North, which is ***inhabited by the Hyperboreans***, who are so named because they dwell beyond the north wind. ***This island is of a happy temperature, rich in soil, and fruitful in every thing, yielding its produce twice in the year.***"

There's no conclusive evidence of agriculture in Finland prior to 500 BC. If Finland were rich in soil, if it were thought of as an island inhabited by Hyperboreans, if it were of a happy temperature, if it were fruitful in everything, and if it yielded its produce twice a year, it would still not be agricultural during the chronology of these civilizations. Next, one must prove how many times of year produce was yielded naturally, but this is subjective because southern Finland's growing season is purportedly two months longer than the season of northern Finland.

Professor Jules Martha claimed that he learned how to read *Liber Linteus* (the Etruscan script wrapping the mummy from Luxor) by using a pattern of affinity he found between the Etruscan script and the Finnish language, which led him to suppose that the Etruscans were an Urgo-Finnish race originating in Russia, near the Ural River.

The northernmost portion of Norway has Inari Sami spoken in it, yet the region is not rich in metals that made Etruscans successful, nor was there any shortage of seafood in Britain or Northern Europe that justified risking one's life to fish there. There's no forest or anything worth colonizing in Honningsvåg in terms of resources demanded by the ancient world. The winters are brutal and deadly once you get close to 50 degrees north latitude. Even with weatherproof gear, it's difficult to handle nighttime outside for more than an hour. The idea of women and children being vulnerable to the elements is unfathomable unless the ancients had some system of survival we're unaware of. There must have been some time allotted for gradually learning how to survive in environments where winter, by most people's standards, lasts more than half of the year. The landscape is inhospitable most of the time. The northern portions of America weren't inhabited year-round, en masse, till the 18th century. Those that lived there part of the year were nomads hunting buffalo, and they are Asiatic like the Nenets people, not Nordic like the Finnish. *Honningsvåg is above 70 degrees north latitude.* The reason I used this region is because that's where the Sami language is spoken, and there are claims about the Phoenicians and Etruscans being descended from the Sami.

Perhaps the connection between the Etrusco-Phoenicians and Northern Europeans, if there is one, is through peopling Britain, then Denmark, the Baltic region, the Scandinavian countries, and then southern Russia (where Etruscan objects were found). Or, it could've been the result of trading in the Black Sea and charting the rivers from there. The name *Russia*, however, is a product of the late Middle Ages, not of Etruria or their nation known as Rasna, the people thus being referred to as Rasnae by some scholars. The Russian alphabet corresponds to Greek letters, which suggests a much later date of diffusion than the period of the Etrusco-Phoenician Empire.

The root of *Rasna* is *Ras*, which is *Res*. It pertains to *head* and *wisdom* in languages like Hebrew (rasit, reshit), Arabic (reis, rais, rashid), Phoenician (res) and the hieroglyphs, as well as *king* (raja) in the Indian languages. The Etruscan language is likely Phoenician, or descended from it, so *Rasnae* would pertain to *lords* or *sages*, people with *wisdom*, not the color red like it does in modern Latinized languages, i.e. roja/rojo, rossa/rosso, etc.

While I don't disagree that there is cultural diffusion, there is no affinity to suggest Etruscan languages or phenotypes originated in Finland or Russia. Uralic languages are confined to a certain geographic region, besides Hungary, that is likely reached by sea. You don't see this with the Etrusco-Phoenician languages. The Italian alphabets, systems of religion, and artifacts are found everywhere they set up marts, some of which are in Northern Europe and Southern Russia. The historical record lacks artifacts and inscriptions that support the idea of Etruscans descending from Finnish people in Russia. Unless archaeological advancements and authentic objects prove otherwise, there will be no evidence to support that claim.

Cyrillic is heavily influenced by Greek, not Etruscan. There's no mystery in the Etrusco-Phoenician words that subsequent cultures use. The diffusion, if not direct descent, is demonstrable. The gods of the Phoenicians and Etruscans are almost identical, with the exceptions being exclusive archetypes, for example, the Etruscan gods *Castor* and *Pollux* (Castur and Pultuce/Pulutuca). Most scholars were of the opinion that the system originated in India and spread to the Occident, but the oldest inscriptions in India are claimed to be the *Mangulam inscriptions* (if you accept their authenticity), which were discovered by Robert Sewell in the caves of a hill in 1882. The location was sacred to the **Jains**, which is significant because the **Jains** use the cross known as the swastika, or gammadion, and there are much earlier versions of this symbol found on Etruscan pottery and gold pendants in Italy, which date to the 8th century BC, over five centuries older than the versions in India. I suspect the archetypes of **Janus** and **Bruma** were brought eastward, from Italy, and through transposition became **Ganesh** and **Brahma**. The word for **monastery**, in India, was **Palli**, which is associated with **Wisdom** in the Occident (Pallas), and this is encoded in names across Europe and the Near East, from **Palatine** Hill (Rome) to **Paladins** and **Palestine**. The earliest known Tamil-Brahmi script only dates to the 3rd century BC, while the *Marsiliana Tablet*, which displays the Etruscan abecedarium, dates to the 9th century BC, making it six centuries older.

When the Zagreb mummy inscription was discovered, scholars thought it was Egyptian script. Jacob Krall noticed it was Etruscan. Nowhere does Mel Copeland mention Finnic or Sami languages in his translation of it. If the Finnic language is the key to understanding Etruscan, why hasn't the world been enlightened and the rest of the Etruscan scripts deciphered? The script (Liber Linteus) is dated to approximately 250 BC on a paleographical guess, but carbon dating indicated the linen textile was manufactured at 390 BC, give or take 45 years. Certain local gods mentioned indicate those who created it were from southeast Tuscany near Lake Trasimeno, where four major Etruscan cities were located: modern day Arezzo, Perugia, Chiusi and Cortona.

Paleography is the study of ancient handwriting. If the dating is accurate, then it means it was written around the middle of the 3rd century BC on linen that was about a century older. This does not make sense. Is there any evidence of people holding onto linens, or any artifact, for several generations only to be used in a funerary rite for some relative they likely wouldn't meet? If all of this were true, then the linen must've been a relic. If the dating isn't accurate, then are the artifacts forgeries, or is the process of dating materials unreliable? I suggest the latter, but it might be both.

The Etruscan languages can't be translated. While words and phrases can be deciphered to give ideas about the subject matter, not enough inscriptions remain, and the ancient languages of Italy are alien to the rest of the world. Yet the alphabets of the rest of the world, all the way to Asia, excluding China and Southeast Asia, descended from Etrusco-Phoenician. I suspect this indicates the Etruscans are much older than recognized, or the empires that history remembers around the turn of the Common Era, including those related to the Greeks and Romans, are much younger and were imagined to be older by historians during the Middle Ages.

Dominique Anziani was kind in his conclusion of Jules Martha's work, "Despite everything, it would be sovereignly unfair not to pay tribute to the colossal labor that represents Mr. Martha's book. If he did not succeed, it was because he could not succeed, and one cannot defend oneself from some sadness by noting that years of work can lead to a complete failure. At least this example should not be lost for Etruscologists. ***They will now know that they have nothing to hope for from the comparison with the Finno-Ugric languages***, or even comparison with other languages as long as these comparisons are not based on foundations which they have hitherto lacked."

I see Jules Martha's work as a total success, because, if we approach it with an earnest scientific mindset, though he tried to prove A caused B, or that Finno-Urgic languages begat Etruscan languages, he ended up proving A does not cause B, i.e., Etruscan languages are not descended from Finno-Urgic languages. We now know this abject fact and needn't spend our energy exploring it anymore. This work may experience the same fate as Jules Martha's work, but it will still be a total success because I established facts. My interpretation of them may be erroneous, and there is a possibility that every object in the archaeological record is forgery, but phenotypes don't lie. Caesar is an Etruscan name, which takes the form of Cesare in modern Italian. For those who can see the patriarch of my family on the cover of this book, the Caesar phenotype was Celtic. Since the Caesar family contributed so much to the Roman Empire around the reckoning of the Common Era, it demonstrates that Etruscans facilitated the Roman Empire's greatness, which, according to Gibbon, gave way to the happiest period of human history, right up to the reign of Commodus.

9 ALLEGED ORIENTALISM

The near-eastern influence climaxed in the 7th century BC. Grant claimed the links established between the Greeks and Etruria was mainly a result of Greek desire for metals, which the Etruscans had. He compared the Etruscans to the modern Japanese, that they were diligent learners, absorbers, and borrowers. Yet, it is still not known how traffic was conducted. (*The Etruscans*, 46.) **Cumae**, which is claimed to be the first ancient Greek colony on mainland Italy, **has ancient non-Greek Etruscan tombs**. The Etruscans were in southern Italy as well. They were not confined to the region labeled Etruria. They were called pirates in a Homeric hymn (VII, 8). Posidonia (Paestum) was located between these trade routes, at the mouth of the River Sele (Silarus). This settlement was partially

Etruscanized to protect their communications with Sybaris. The paintings at Posidonia are identical with those of a south-Etruscan group. (Grant, Ib. p. 48.) If Posidonia (Paestum) was Etruscanized, might it be that we are looking at the cover-up of an ancient empire, one that scholars claimed to be of Greek origin rather than Etrusco-Phoenician?

Plato wrote of Greek cities (Phaedo, 109B), "We live round the sea like ants and frogs around a pond." This was a characteristic of the Etruscans. The Tyrrhenian Sea received its name due to the command of the seas that the Etruscans had. *Tyrrhenian* (Tyrsenian) is a Greek word for these Italians, whereas the Latins called them *Hetrusci*. According to Pliny the Elder (NH, VII, 56, 209) the invention of ships' beaks is credited to Pisaeus, the mythological the son of Tyrrhenus, an archetypal *Etruscan*. The root of this word is found in the capital of Phoenicia (Tyre), as well as the Norse god of war (Tyr). *Tyre* is spelled *tsadi-resh* (Tsr) in Phoenician, pronounced *Sur*. This word is the root of the Indian *Surya*, as well as the Etruscan *Suri* (Hades) and the Norse *Surtr*. It is also the root of *Syrian* and *Assyrian*. *Sur* is philologically *sar*, which is present in *Aesar*, *Tsar*, *Czar*, *Caesar*, and much more.

Etruscan pottery was found at Samos. (M. Gras, Mél. Heurgon, I, p. 364.) The *Lemnos Stele* is similar to the reliefs of *Alve Feluske* at Vetulonia and *Avle Tite* at Volaterrae. There are other Lemnian fragments that are indecipherable, but the letters and language are similar to Etruscan. The people from Thessaly (northern Greece) were thought to be the original settlers of Lemnos. They were identified with Tyrsenians or Tyrrhenians (Etruscans) according to Grant. (Ib. p 57.) Thucydides wrote of people on the adjacent mainland, claiming they were "of Tyrrhenian race". He added that *this was the race that once lived in Lemnos—and Athens!* Grant claimed this last detail about Athens was invented by Thucydides's source because it was convenient for Athenian politicians to legitimize the forcible seizure of the island in c. 500 BC, but there may be something more to the account. The evidence mentioned was previously used to craft a narrative that Etruscans came from the Orient. But I suspect it is the exact opposite and that history was inverted. I suspect the Etrusco-Phoenicians civilized the Greeks and there was a cover-up of the ancient maritime empire, whose epicenter was Italy. It's a clever way of reifying Mosaic history, which was used by the religious institutions and nobility to derive their lineages and justify their divine right to rule.

In light of the Tuscaloosa Indians in Mississippi using the Sicilian Phoenician symbol of the open hand with an eye in its palm, also reimagined and named by younger cultures as the *hamsa* symbol, the languages of America ought to be examined with greater scrutiny. The word *papalotl* means *butterfly* in Classical Nahuatl, the Aztec lingua franca during the time of Spanish arrival. *Papilio* is the Latin word for *butterfly*. *Is this coincidence?* If the Nahuatl termination is removed, then it becomes the same word. I wouldn't claim the Nahuatl language has affinity to Latin, but if two more identical words are found between the two, then the odds become 10 to 1 that they were introduced by the same source, or that the languages descend from the same source. If ten philologically identical words can be found between the two languages, then those odds jump to 100,000 to 1 in favor of diffusion. *Teotl* is a term for **sacredness** or **divinity** in Mexico, sometimes used for **God**. This is similar to the Roman-Gaulic **Toutatis**, or **Tot**, the Egyptian **Thoth**, and the Greek **Theos**, all associated with **God** and the archetypes of **Mars** and **Mercury** (Hermes). **Toutatis** was also spelled **Teutates**, which begat the name **Teutons**, ascribed to Germanic people.

Phoenicians allegedly gave the Greeks a 17-letter alphabet, yet the oldest abecedarium that was claimed to be ancient Greek turned out to be Etruscan. The *Marsiliana tablet* has more than 17 letters. Greek is an Indo-European language. Etruscan is not. There is a prevalence of fatalism in Italian culture. It can inspire men to achieve great accomplishments but it can also inspire them to accept terrible outcomes. The cause of this outlook among the ancient Italians is difficult to determine. In other cultures, for example, Southeast Asia or China, worldviews can be attributed to a belief in reincarnation. Etruscan art is not realistic. It is fantastic, sometimes grotesque, and more akin to Picasso. It proves they were not Greek. According to Grant (Ib. p.60), the Etruscans believed they were under the thumb of divine power, which made them uninterested in idealizing the male and female forms like the Greeks did. "In spite of its habitual connections with Greece, *the art of Etruria is really very little Greek*." (Brendel, p. 305; M. I. Finley, Aspects of Antiquity (1968), p. 110.)

The Etruscans were fond of Gorgons, which are usually depicted like suns. I suspect these are the origin of the sun-devil symbolism, as well as the serpent symbolism incorporated into the Nagas of India. Etruscan temples were different than Greek ones and were closer to near-eastern styles. The shapes of their tombs differed from those of the Greek variety, and, unlike the Etruscans, the Greeks didn't have wall paintings in tombs. Etruscan statues were exclusively funerary and not made of stone but of terracotta (baked earth), which makes me wonder if they learned this art from the Chinese or if this technique was brought to China from the Mediterranean. Reference the terracotta army found in one of the forty Chinese pyramids (most of which haven't been excavated yet).

The Etruscans used the ***bucchero*** technique in making ceramics, not the red-figure vases that were prevalent in Greece. Etruscan bronze figures also differ from Greek ones. The Etruscans brought filigree techniques to an unprecedented degree of refinement and employed granulation to render figures in outline or silhouette in a way never encountered in Greece. (Grant. Ib. p. 62.) ***Filigree*** is from the Latin ***filum***, meaning ***thread***, and ***granum***, meaning ***grain***, in the sense of a small bead.

All the jewelry of the Etruscans and Greeks, that wasn't intended for the grave, was made by soldering the material together to build the gold up, rather than chiseling or engraving the material. Approximately ten thousand Etruscan inscriptions were found, but only four or five of them are more than one hundred words long. Only about a dozen contain more than thirty words. Yet, what does remain provides the best example of contrast between the Etruscans and the Greeks. Grant acknowledged specialists resent the fact that Etruscan cannot be translated. (Ib. p. 66.) He wrote, *"The structure of the language is, so far, not recognized or understood—that is to say, despite the advances achieved by various methods of interpretation, we still do not even know the linguistic group to which it belongs, or the other languages, if any, which may be related to it."*

Etruscan belongs to no other linguistic group. According to Massimo Pallottino, *Etruscan was a language 'whose origin is basically non-Indo-European, or at least whose structure cannot be described in terms that are typical of the Indo-European languages'.* (Pallottino, Etr, p. 53.) According Dionysius of Halicarnassus, *Etruscan was unlike all known languages.* (DH, I. 29, 1, 1.) They allegedly formed a separate nation called *Rasna* or *Rasnae*, transliterated by the Greeks as *Rasenna*. (G. Radke, *Klio*, LVI (1974), p. 303. The name originated from north-eastern Etruria; see J. Heurgon, Archeologica: scritti in onore di Aldo Neppi Modona, pp. 353-8.)

How could a language that is not a member of any other language's linguistic group possess the Pelasgic alphabet, which is the same as the Phoenician one? The three Indo-European languages of Italy were claimed to be *Latin and Sicel* (eastern Sicily), *Umbro-Sebellian*, and *Messapian* (southeastern Italy). But I'm not sure about this because some historians, such as Pliny the Elder, claimed the Umbrians were the oldest culture in Italy. If the Umbrians were oldest, then how could their language conform to Indo-European? These details are disputable and the answer is obvious. The native languages of Italy are alien to the rest of the world, yet their alphabets are used by the rest of the world and are synonymous with Pelasgic, an alphabet that is of Phoenician original. The Etruscans were called Pelasgians, thus, the Phoenicians were indigenous to Italy and are either the ancestors or descendants of the Etruscans, if not a term assigned to the Etruscan navigators.

The Indo-European influence appeared to stop at the Tiber River, where the languages beyond it were non-Indo-European. Among these were the ancient *Ligurian*, *Raetian*, *Sardinian*, *Sican* (western Sicily), and the *Etruscan* languages, all indigenous to Italy. If the Sicans were at Mount Alban, then it's another way of being connected to, or being part of, the Phoenicians. This is accounted by the Phoenician history in Sicily. If they are associated with the Pelasgians, then it is another detail that identifies the Phoenicians as ancient Italians.

Greeks and Romans only mentioned the Etruscans when there were significant events involving them, such as skirmishes. They appear in classical literature in an ancillary capacity, usually in a negative context of being alien and hostile. But many of these writers (such as Cicero) were involved with or sympathetic to the treachery that ruined Roman culture and Italy as a whole. Grant touched upon the technique (Ib. p. 72.), where the Greeks and Romans created imaginary origins of peoples and cities, based on mythology and astrotheology, not on archaeological evidence. Herodotus's informants invented a connection between the Tyrrhenians and Lydians on account of a town called Tyrrha, suggesting the Etruscans (Tyrrhenians) came from Lydia, which is Asia Minor or modern-day Turkey. The Greeks also attempted to link the Etruscans to a group of people from Thyrion (Thyrium) in northwestern Greece, called Dardanians, named after being descended from King Dardanus of Troy, a mythological archetype that transferred to Italy under the guise of Tyrrhus, the shepherd and King of the Latins. But the Etruscans were not shepherds. Some of their towns had no agricultural centers. They were a maritime people once they advanced beyond primitive living. There is no ethnic or etymological connection between the Dardanians and the Etruscans. (Grant. Ib. p. 74.) Dionysius of Halicarnassus also exposed the Greek mythological imperialism (I, 30, 1), "I do not believe that the Tyrrhenians (Etruscans) were a colony of the Lydians. For *they do not use the same language* as the latter, *nor can it be alleged* that, though they no longer speak a similar tongue, they nevertheless still retain some other indications of their mother country. For *they neither worship the same gods as the Lydians nor make use of similar laws or institutions.*"

The evidence indicates that the Etruscans were Phoenicians who were indigenous to Italy. The suggestion that the Etruscans were a people driven to Etruria by Iron Age invaders from the east, or anywhere else, is implausible because everywhere they settled is the best land with the best resources, and this is not consistent with reality. Nowhere do we see people driven from their homeland and forced to settle better lands. Settling better land only happens through exploration and conquest.

10 ETRUSCAN ROME

Grant confirmed the phenotype of the Etrusco-Romans was not Oriental by explaining that the culture of Italy and Etruria, before and after 1000 BC, had a central European appearance rather than an east European one. (The Etr. p. 78.) Some scholars use this very fact to claim the Etruscans came to Italy from across the Alps, an idea supported by the introduction of cremation tombs, which housed urns filled with the ashes of the dead. They were arranged in cemeteries known as urnfields, the oldest of which were concentrated in the Tolfa-Allumiere region. The Italian urnfields are similar to the urnfields of the Danubian area, a civilization that was known for their urnfield culture in the second millennium BC. The Danubian region possessed vital commodities such as copper and salt. But there is a detail in Italian archaeology that debunks the notion of Danubian migration into Italy. Although cremation in urnfields prevailed across the Alps, it is not certain that this was the route in which the custom arrived in Italy. The archaeological evidence suggests that **urnfield culture spread from south to north** in Italy, which, in addition to the elements of Etruscan lifestyles, indicates **there is no evidence of mass migration into Etruria from the north or the east just before or after the end of the 2nd millennium BC.**

If the archaeological record can be depended on, it leaves two options regarding what occurred in the 2nd millennium BC: either Italy was colonized by maritime endeavors from some advanced culture like the Phoenicians (it can't be the Greeks due to the alienness of the language), or the Etruscans are original Europeans who were indigenous to Italy and became an advanced maritime culture on account of their location, a culture that is now referred to as the Phoenicians. The primitive living structures in the archaeological record are present to demonstrate this natural Italian progression. Could this migration have occurred thousands of years prior? Of course, but the aim of this work is not to deal with the origins of prehistoric people. According to Cristofani (Etr. p. 75), cited by Grant, "Though language does not necessarily coincide with race or racial movements, the presence of many Italian loan-words and names in Etruscan suggests that **the Etruscan language was at home in Italy for some time before c. 700 BC.**"

The Etruscans had an un-Greek view of the afterlife. (Grant, Ib. pp. 64, 65.) While the historical record indicates that Greeks believed in life after death (an obvious stereo-type fallacy, but generalization serves a function here), there is nothing to suggest their views were comparable to the conviction of the Etruscans that death was not a real break in continuity at all, but a prolongation and perpetuation of life on earth, which is the motivation behind their tombs. The wealth stored in the chambers of the tombs is more akin to the practices of the ancient Egyptians than that of the Greeks, and the colorful Etruscan wall paintings, the most impressive ones discovered thus far being Tarquinian, are un-Greek. It may turn out that the Etruscans are descended from the pre-dynastic Egyptians, or that the pre-dynastic Egyptians are descended from the Etruscans, but then that would imply the pre-dynastic Egyptians were Celtic, not Asiatic as they are pretended to be.

The Etruscans founded Capua around 800 BC according to Velleius Paterculus (I, 7, 2-4). It is different from the rest of the Etrurian cities because it was founded on level ground, which is more akin to towns in the region of Campania, located in the middle of agricultural territory. Capua is far beyond the border of Etruria. Ceramics produced by Greek craftsmen at Pithecusae and Cumae were found there, but they are identical with those found in Etruria. Does this indicate Capua was Greek and then Etruscanized, or is it an example of Etruscan pottery being attributed to Greeks, much like their letters were? Archaeologists have not produced evidence to determine when Capua became Etruscan.

According to Pliny the Elder (Pliny, *NH*, III, 5, 70.), the Picentine region, now called Pontecagnano, was Etruscan. It is located southeast of Naples, which has Greek influence, yet its Etruscan character dates back to the 9th century BC, corroborated by objects found in its cemeteries, which indicates that it was in communication with Etruria, if not an Etruscan colony. The site is virtually indistinguishable from those of Etruria in the same period, but there were seventh-century vases, brooches, cups, and an inscription *from Phoenicia* found in wealthy tombs dated to c. 700 BC. Are these items from Phoenicia, or are they ancient Italian artifacts being attributed to their colonies in Phoenicia? Excavations at Rome produced objects of Egypto-Phoenician appearance dating from before and after 600 BC, of precisely the types that Pithecusae and Cumae were exporting extensively to the Etruscans. (Grant, Ib. pp. 93, 94.) The drying-out of the Roman Forum in the same period that was effected by the construction of an impressive drain, the *Cloaca Maxima*, was an Etruscan technique. At the same time, the first pottery and metalwork from the nearest cities of southern Etruria appeared at Rome (a tomb on the Esquiline Hill was found to contain Etruscan-type armour dated to about 600 BC). Rome was an Etruscan colony and dependent, but it also had its own unique Etruscan-type culture. Look no further than the name of one of its ancient streets: *Vicus Tuscus* (Etruscan Street). It was near *Capitoline Hill*, which still has statues of the Etruscan gods Castor and Pollux. The origins of *Vicus Tuscus* aren't known for certain since there are conflicting historical accounts. The Etruscans influenced Roman culture, artifacts, and irrigation techniques. It is claimed that an image and shrine of Venus Cloacina was found in the so-called drainage system (*Cloaca Maxima*; Greatest Sewer), but it may have served as a labyrinth or canal system prior to being built upon. Venus generally invokes the sea and the sea people, also known as Venetians and Phoenicians, which would be another indication of the Phoenicians and Venetians being Etruscan navigators. Since another way of writing Etruscan is *Tuscus*, did the Tuscaloosa Indians in Mississippi take their name after them? How did they receive or learn about the Sicilian and Carthaginian hamsa symbol, found on their *Rattlesnake Disk*? Or, is the *Rattlesnake Disk* a modern work inspired by ancient cultures and pretended to be older? The burial mounds in America appear similar to Etruscan tumuli on the surface, but lack the stone architecture to indicate diffusion.

According to Grant (Ib. pp. 94, 95.), Rome was Etruscanized but consisted of Italic-speaking communities. *Sant'Omobono* contained sixth-century Etruscan statues. The temple of Jupiter, Juno and Minerva (Tinia, Uni and Menrva to the Etruscans) was the largest temple of the Etruscan style and form ever built. The formula of its triple structure was found in other Etruscan cities, and Etruscan sculptures made by Vulca of Veii decorated it. Rome's institutions embodied Etruscan features. Etruscans influenced Roman religion, mythology, their calendar, ceremonial customs, agriculture, art, and costumes. The same can be said of the Phoenicians influencing the Etruscans, which may indicate that Roman history is Etrusco-Phoenician history, and much of the conflict over territory in the Mediterranean was akin to civil war.

11 VOLATERRAE & CLUSIUM

Volaterrae

There is a relief claimed to be **Triton** (a Greek archetype) on a funerary urn found in Volaterrae, dated to the 2nd century BC. However, Triton is not usually depicted with wings on artifacts, and the Volaterrae archetype looks like it has female breasts, the details of which have faded over time. If my assessment is accurate, then I suspect this is an Etruscan version of **Echidna** or some other aquatic serpentine archetype. Volaterrae was known to provide ships' rigging and grain to the Roman fleet as late as 205 BC. An Etruscan city-state having this kind of responsibility for one of the greatest empires is demonstrative of their nautical capabilities, which must have existed for a long time prior. There are prominent themes of sirens and *Uturze* (Uthurze), an equivalent to the Roman *Ulysses* and the Greek *Odysseus*, on funerary urns at the location. The Volaterreans were a maritime people. Little is known about them beyond that. Could it be because they were Phoenicians? Those who spent their lives taking to the high seas are not likely to leave much behind on land.

Maritime and serpentine archetypes such as *Triton, Uturze, Ulysses, Odysseus, Echidna, Melusina, Typhon*, and the like, are depicted in opposite parts of the world. I suspect it is cultural diffusion. *Nüwa*, also read *Nügua*, is a mother goddess and alleged member of the Three Sovereigns of Chinese mythology. She is a god in Chinese folk religion and Taoism, and is credited with creating humanity and repairing the Pillar of Heaven. This symbolism could also be connected to the *Nagas*, which are divine, or semi-divine, half-human and half-serpent archetypes that reside in the netherworld (Patala). The feminine form is called a *Nagi*, or a *Nagini*.

The leading family of Volaterrae for most of its history was the Ceicna (Caecina) clan, which owned extensive lands, including clay-pits, kilns, and salt-pans. They named the adjoining river or took their name from it. Four tombs inscribed with their names have come to light at Volaterrae, one containing no less than forty cremation urns. (Grant, The Etr. p. 195.) The estuary of the Cecina River had a Roman port three miles north of it called Vada Volaterrana. This may have been the Etrusco-Phoenician port used by the locals, which the Romans inherited.

According to my contacts in Italy, there are many locations in the country that the locals have no idea about who existed prior, but they are aware of subsequent cultures building on top of older cities. There are plenty of locations dating to the Roman Empire that haven't been excavated yet. We are in the early stages of discovery. Archaeology is a skillset that gets better as technology and techniques improve, and one can only hope that archaeologists will refrain from forgery as more discoveries are made. One of the keys to understanding Volaterrae will be the Arno River, which was likely an important route for connecting Etruscan culture and facilitating commerce. The Volaterrans would've accessed it first, which is likely how they developed their maritime prowess.

According to Polybius (III, 79, 8.), "The Arno basin was not by any means easy to exploit, since broad waterlogged marshlands extended across the almost level plain on both its banks, especially in spring-time after the floods: in the third century BC *it took the Carthaginian Hannibal*, invading Italy, *four days to cross these marshes.*"

If the knowledge of these subjects advances, it'll reveal several layers of history that were lost and will shed more light on the founding of Florence. There are also rivers beside the Arno such as the Era, where Etruscan objects were found, such as iron from Elba, likely by way of Volaterrae. Etruscan tombs were also found in Terricciola. There were artifacts, such as a bronze mirror, excavated at Monteriggioni. The tomb of La Montagnola survived almost intact. There were many Etruscan artifacts and tombs discovered in places that were also Ligurian, which leads me to suspect these cultures were not separate or divided as believed by historians. The horseshoe-shaped gravestones from c. 510 BC, found in Bononia, resemble those of Faesulae and commemorate the Caecina family, who were prominent at Volaterrae. (Grant. Ib. p. 201.) This investigation has barely begun, and whether I become a part of it or not, I suspect future discoveries will uncover the connections between an ancient Italian empire that became nautical and expanded around the world.

Clusium

Clusium's art emphasized grotesque but not necessarily repulsive forms. It is reminiscent of sculptures found in Sardegna. They also implemented the use of sarcophagi, which may indicate a strong relationship with Egypt. The people of Clusium were fond of decorating urns and jars with human heads as lids. Their city walls are only 64 acres and indicate that they did not farm inside of it, meaning they were not an agricultural city-state. Unfortunately, most of the information known about them is mostly found in their cemeteries and tombs.

The *Situla of the Pania*, an ivory situla or pyxis from the end of the 7th century BC, was found in the *Tomb of the Pania* at Clusium. It is one of the only examples of Etruscan ivory work, the others being from the same place, and one from Cerveteri. The upper frieze shows two myths from the *Odyssey*, split by a sphinx: the encounter with **Scylla** (who looks a lot like a hydra) and the escape from Polyphemus (a Cyclops). The second frieze shows departure for war, followed by hoplites saluting, and then weeping women, a warrior without his shield performing a funerary dance, and then a horseman. The third band displays beasts and monsters. The final band depicts imaginary animals.

There was also a silver vase of unknown origin found there. Some think it is from Caere while others think it is from Phoenicia, but Grant suggested that its northern situla form indicates its place of origin may be Clusium, where it was found. (The Etruscans, p. 203.)

The Chiana valley was renown for its grain. It was made possible due to its expansive irrigation that was provided by the Etruscans of Clusium, which limited the floodwaters of the river and gave way to an intricate system of trenches, tunnels, and other channels. (Grant, Ib. p. 206.) There were pastures northeast of the shores of Lake Trasimeno, and the lake was abundant in fish, birds, and reeds. In addition, it enabled easy maritime communication. These qualities facilitated a dense rural population in the area ruled by Clusium.

The Clusines established major settlements in their territory more than any other Etruscan people. The settlements became thriving independent centers on account of their prosperity. One of them was Arretium (Arezzo). Strabo described Arretium as the farthest inland of all the towns of Etruria (V, 2, 9, 226). It was approximately 30 miles away. Etruscan remains on a hill next to San Donatus indicate the acropolis San Cornelio was an Etruscan fort. Other significant finds in Arezzo include the necropolis *Poggio del Sole* (the Hill of the Sun), the famous *Chimera of Arezzo* (5th century BC), as well as the *Minerva of Arezzo* (the dates on this conflict; c. 4th-2nd century BC).

The Arrentines specialized in bronze-work, but it is unclear whether they specialized in this trade prior to Arezzo's urbanization. The industry grew as a result of supplying Gauls, or whoever the people in northern Italy were, with arms. Red pottery is found all over Europe, and even though it was made after Rome possessed Arezzo, the pottery is called *Arretine* (terra sigillata) because it was mass-produced there.

Cortona was between Clusium and Arretium. It was rich in foundation myths, but they are of late origin and based on false etymological analogies. (Grant, Ib. p. 209.) Confusion with Croton was the cause of the strange story that the Greek philosopher Pythagoras, of Samos, came to Cortona. Monumental mound tombs appeared in Cortona in the 7th century BC, known as **meloni**. The largest mound tomb is the *Melone di Camucia*, which is similar to *Newgrange* in Ireland.

Even under "Roman" rule, the Perusians continued to build magnificent tombs inscribed with Etrusco-Phoenician letters. The *Ipogeo dei Volumni*, or Hypogeum of the Volumnus family, is an Etruscan tomb in Ponte San Giovanni, which is a suburb of Perugia, Umbria, located in central Italy. Archaeologists do not know when the tomb was created, but some speculate it dates to the 3rd century BC. According to the chronology related to the founding of Rome, it means that, despite Roman expansion, these people were still speaking Etruscan. Even the Umbrian alphabet is Etruscan, with minimal variation. This contradicts claims of the Umbrians being the oldest civilization in Italy, or it indicates that the Etrusco-Phoenicians descend from the Umbrians, which doesn't make sense given that it is located in the middle of the country. This supports my suspicion that the history of "Rome", prior to the Common Era, is one of Etruria and was misrepresented by Common Era historians, something that continues in the present day. The lack of knowledge about the ancient Italians and their alienness to the rest of the world are marks of their antiquity rather than their youth.

One of Clusium's farthest outposts was Murlo (Poggio Civitate). Grant claimed it wasn't possible that Perusia took part in the northern expansion of Etruria. He explained that Bononia (modern Bologna), which was called Felsina in Etruscan, was named after a Clusine family, the Felsnal. (Ib. p. 215.) It appears that Clusium took over the operations of expanding north from Volaterrae around the beginning of the 6th century BC, but it is uncertain whether this shift took place by decree or by natural growth. While Volaterrae's presence didn't cease, the archaeological evidence suggests that the Clusines were more active in the area following this period. Thus, the Clusines and the people north of the Apennines influenced each other in art and other ways of life, specifically the alphabet, a secret system not available to the masses at the time. This implies an interconnected priesthood and aristocracy.

Marzabotto is linked with Clusium more than anywhere else. The Etruscans from Clusium settled to the north, in places like

Marzabotto, and to the south, all the way down to Campania. There was a road connection between these locations, but Virgil claimed there was a maritime connection, which would've required an alliance with Vulci. This might be difficult to rectify because scholars are under the impression that Vulci and Clusium clashed over control of the metals in two areas on Mount Amiata. If Clusium had access to the sea, then it means there wasn't constant hostility between the regions as supposed. But the lack of certainty highlights how little is known about Etruria, which ought not to be the case if the Etruscans are younger than the Greeks.

As the empire expanded inland, it brought its system all over Europe, and I suspect this is why the Scandinavians, Germans, and the like, use Italian alphabets and systems of religion and governance. They are remnants of a culture, not strangers who were introduced to the systems through commerce, conquest, and priestcraft. It should also be noted that **Lars** and **Porsenna** may be titles of rank or glory, and not a so-called King of Clusium, but whomever this individual was, known as **Lars Porsenna**, Macaulay claimed the banner of Clusium was the highest of them all under his rule. (*Lays of Ancient Rome.*) There is farrago regarding Lars Porsenna conquering Rome, as well as being repelled from Rome in his attempt to conquer it. The rest of the history regarding Clusium, and how it became absorbed by Rome during the Romano-Etruscan period, remains uncertain. Esteemed scholars conceded the details of the Gauls, Clusines, and Romans appear legendary and mythological.

12 VEII & MURLO

I cited Godfrey Higgins in *Spirit Whirled*, highlighting the problem with the locations alleged to be Veii. He wrote, "Three places near Rome are clearly proved by inscriptions to have been the site of this celebrated town. Has God multiplied the ruins of cities for the amusement of antiquarians, as the author was told in Italy, that he has multiplied the heads of dead saints for the edification of the faithful?"

It might be that none of the locations claiming to be Veii are the ancient city. The *Ponte Sodo* at Veii, an artificially enlarged tunnel, what Grant called a characteristic masterpiece of Etruscan hydraulic engineering, channeled the *Fosso Valchetta* (River Cremera) through a rocky outcrop so as to prevent flooding and assist irrigation.

The *Tomb of the Roaring Lions* is located at the accepted site of Veii. It has well-preserved fresco paintings of four feline creatures, which are believed to be lions, but one must consider the fantastical nature of Etruscan art. If they wanted to depict realistic creatures, they could have. But they preferred the surreal. The tomb is one of the oldest painted tombs in the western Mediterranean, dating back to 690 BC. The awareness of it was only made public in 2006 by a tombarolo (illegal excavator) in exchange for a lenient sentence from his charges of trafficking illegally excavated antiquities. Etruscan artifacts are scattered abroad based on this black market trade, causing their provenance to become lost.

Dionysius of Halicarnassus described Veii being equivalent to Athens in size (II, 54), "The third war Romulus engaged in was against **the most powerful city of the Tyrrhenian race** at that time, called **Veii**, distant from Rome about a hundred stades; it is situated on a high and craggy rock and is **as large as Athens**. The Veientes made the taking of Fidenae the pretext for this war, and sending ambassadors, they bade the Romans withdraw their garrison from that city and restore to its original possessors the territory they had taken from them and were now occupying. And when their demand was not heeded, they took the field with a great army and established their camp in a conspicuous place near Fidenae."

Grant claimed Falerii (modern day Civita Castellana) may be regarded as a kind of extension of Veii and, at its height, was in some respects as important a city and state (or state capital) as the purely Etruscan centers, or Rome itself at the same period. (Ib. p. 227.) The name *Faliscans*, ascribed to the people of Falerii, is philologically similar to **Pelasgians** and **Phoenicians**, but the detail, as of now, is anecdotal.

One of the primary achievements that will lead a people out of a nomadic lifestyle is the discovery of salt and its use for preserving food. The Veientines relied on the salt-beds at the mouth of the Tiber River and the Tyrrhenian Sea. They prospered as a result of their situation because salt did not appear in similar quantities anywhere else in Etruria. The Carthaginians settled locations near natural salt-pans in North Africa, Sardegna, and Spain as a result of this achievement, whether it is an Etruscan discovery or not.

If Dionysius of Halicarnassus can be depended on for historical accounts, the salt-beds of Veii were so significant that their forced abandonment was a condition imposed by the Romans on the Veientines to ensure submission. He wrote (II, 55, 5), "This was the third triumph that Romulus celebrated, and it was much more magnificent than either of the former. And when, not long afterwards, ambassadors arrived from the Veientes to seek an end to the war and to ask pardon for their offenses, Romulus imposed the following penalties upon them: to deliver up to the Romans the country adjacent to the Tiber, called the Seven Districts, and ***to abandon the salt-works near the mouth of the river***, and also to bring fifty hostages as a pledge that they would attempt no uprising in the future."

The salting and preservation of meats would've been useful, if not necessary, for a maritime empire. With the name **Faliscans** being similar to *Pelasgians* and *Phoenicians*, even if you remove their terminations or Latinize them, i.e., *Falisci, Pelasgi*, and *Fenici* or *Punici*, I suspect the missing component that eludes scholars and historians is the likelihood of a universal empire from Italy that thrived before the Roman one. Carthaginians are a branch of Phoenicians whose language is from Sicily and called Punic. North Africa, Sardegna, and Spain (before it lost the use of letters under the Goths) were branches of the Phoenicians. The chieftain of the proto-Celtic Lusitanians from western Hispania, located on the Iberian Peninsula, was called Punicus by Roman chroniclers, implying he served the Phoenicians or was descended from them. This detail is one of many that indicate the Phoenicians were Celtic. The Basque people, just north of Hispania Lusitania, speak Spanish Phoenician, which still uses Etruscan words like *aita*. I imagine the reason the Faliscan region didn't have a port is because it didn't need one. It was part of the Etrusco-Phoenician Empire and its primary function was to provide salt for its navigators as they explored the rest of the world. After an alleged war with the Romans, the Faliscans were relocated to a place that could not be defended, the present day Santa Maria di Falleri.

Narce (now Calcata) was further south of Falerii, in the valley of Treia, or Treja, which is philologically Troia (Troy). The Etruscans chose excellent locations for their towns, where the landscape aided in their defense, which is why the Romans relocated them. It's another detail that proves they didn't migrate or flee to Italy. Nearby was Soracte (Mount Soratte), the site of a sanctuary of Feronia, an

Italian goddess whose name may be Etruscan. Soracte was situated at a cross-roads between the east and west of the Tiber river. As mentioned by Dionysius of Halicarnassus, Veii had an outpost on Latian soil, only five miles north of Rome, called Fidenae (Castel Giubileo). However, no traces of buildings or fortifications from the ancient world are to be seen in Fidenae, which is problematic given the three different cities that claimed to be Veii.

The *Bernardini Tomb*, which produced an inscription recording a form of an ancient Veientine royal name, **Vetusia**, was in the same region. (Grant, Ib. p. 230.) The artifacts found at the *Bernardini Tomb* may indicate the Etruscans are Phoenician, as archaeologists refer to one of the objects as the *Phoenician bowl*. Perhaps it's an Etruscan bowl and the objects they've called "Phoenician" are Etruscan.

Romans relied on Veii for their cultural model. The archaeological record, unearthed at Rome, reveals Veientine bucchero pottery and metalwork dating to c. 625 BC onwards. Identical terracotta friezes were discovered, placed about a century later. Vulca of Veii was employed by Romans to make the statue of Jupiter for the temple that the Etrusco-Roman monarchs erected for Jupiter, Juno, and Minerva. The cult of Aeneas is recorded nearby at Politorium, which some think may have come from Veii rather than directly from Vulci. There is a possibility that the Roman bronze-work, known as the *Capitoline Wolf*, was made by a pupil of Vulca in the second quarter of the 5th century BC, but B. Andreae was of the opinion that the work was un-Etruscan. (Grant, Ib. p. 230.)

One of the Etruscan religious institutions that Rome adopted was the priesthood of Mars, known as the Salian order. It was allegedly formed by the Veinentine King Morrius, or by the armorer Mamurius Veturius (whose name is related to Vetusia), and then introduced by King **Numa**, whose name is **Amun** when read like Etruscan. **Amun** finds its way into **Baal Hammon**, **Jupiter Ammon**, **Zeus Ammon**, and **Jesus the Amen**. These figures are mythological in appearance, with Mamurius Veturius being similar to Vulcan, which also makes Vulca appear mythological. Is King **Morrius** the Phoenician origin of **Mars**? **Maur** is a Phoenician word meaning **great**, **lord**, or **prince**, still used by Italians in names like **Mauro**. It was also used by the British and Gaulish kings, i.e., **Condomarus**, **Cwismarus**, **Combolomarus**, **Induciomarus**, **Viridomarus**, **Teutomarus**. **Maru** was an Etruscan title and part of Virgil's full name.

Grant believed the wars began as a result of the end of the Etruscan kings of Rome. (Ib. p. 231.) The most ancient of the conflicts should not be admitted into the historical record because Roman historians imagined them. The Roman Republic was allegedly under the control of the Fabii in the 5th century BC, who possessed links with Etruria. Grant suggested they owned land in the direction of Veii, which is why they were entrusted with the defense of the Veientine frontier. The Fabii protected this frontier with a private semi-feudal army like those found in Etruria and Greece at the time.

Certain Etruscan sites are not mentioned in ancient historical or epigraphical texts (inscriptions on statues or edifices). The same can be said of ancient British sites. Why were they not noticed? Could it be because they're chronologically modern? Is it because they are so ancient that they had long ceased to exist by the time Roman and Greek chroniclers would've accounted for them? Is it possible that most of the work pertaining to Roman and Greek writers are forgeries created by the priests during the Middle Ages?

Kyle Phillips noted that the site of Poggio Civitate was destroyed in an intentional and ritualistic manner on account of the construction of the mound and the burial of the architectural decoration away from the building. This idea, though logical, doesn't demonstrate anything. What classifies as destruction? What if a port was partially destroyed by a natural disaster, or an act of war, and, in order to restore function, the rest of the location had to be destroyed? What if the sites were destroyed after becoming dilapidated? The history of these locations is a contested subject among archaeologists and Etruscologists.

According to Edlund-Berry (*Mur. Etr.* pp. 22, 24.), early cults at the sanctuary of Gravisca, the harbor town of Tarquinia, included the worship of Aphrodite, Hera, Demeter, and Apollo. They were replaced by Etruscan cults in the 5th and 4th centuries BC, including a healing cult in the 4th century BC. A shift took place around the 4th century BC and the old cults were replaced, transformed, or augmented through the introduction of the healing cults. However, without written evidence, there is no way to tell what models the Etruscans followed in determining whether a site should be abandoned or rebuilt. These healing cults caused a major change in both beliefs and practices in Etruria and Central Italy, as well as new deities to be introduced throughout the Roman Republic along with the construction of temples in their honor. I suspect the foundations of the new system were laid at this time, which eventually became the Universal, or Catholic, Church. *Æsculapius* and *Jesus* are both gods of healing and miracle work, thus *Therapeutae* or *Essenes* signify *healers* and *miracle workers*, whose writings Eusebius admitted were the Christian gospels and epistles.

Kyle Phillips claimed that, of the pottery found at Poggio Civitate, only a tiny group of the Greek or Greek-inspired pots may be isolated as imports. The majority of them were of local manufacture (Mur. Etr. p. 29.), indicating they are of Etruscan origin. According to Wikander (Mur. Etr. p. 61.), there were fifteen Etruscan lateral simas found, and as many as six belong to the same type, some possibly from the same mold, which date to c. 530 BC. They represent the last phase of the local Etruscan terracotta industry, but this detail begets a mystery because *there is no successor to this industry* in the archaeological record. The terracotta roofs are followed by roofs with shell antefixes along the eaves. Wikander explained the abrupt end of the terracotta industry was due to the emergence of large temples with unprecedented dimensions, which the existing terracotta types were not suitable for. (Ib. p. 62.) As a result of the finds at Poggio Civitate, *there is no longer any reason to look for inspiration in Ionia*. (Mur. Etr. p. 63.) On the contrary, if there is a connection with Sardis, Neandria, Düver, etc., the chronological factors indicate an influence *from Etruria* to Ionia regarding revetment plaques.

The diffusion, if there is any, is likely the result of Etruscan Thalassocrats, who, for lack of a better term (since each city-state is unique), are remnants of the Phoenician or Pelasgian mariners, if not the very navigators themselves. The best Etruscologists, though none of them publicly suspected this, demonstrated the un-Greek nature of the Etruscans. This indicates that Dionysius of Halicarnassus's explanation of the Pelasgians is implausible. They could not have been a race of Greeks who fled to Etruria, only to be expelled by the Etruscans. Nowhere is the Etrusco-Phoenician alienness more apparent than in their indigenous Italian languages, which are claimed to be Pelasgic.

13 DISMANTLING THE DEMARATIAN NARRATIVE

Italy was a hub of the world. Though it appears several races lived there and made it their home, there is an indigenous Italian system responsible for the civilization of the world over the last several thousand years. According to Grant (The Etr. p. 238.), *it is misleading to insist on the Greekness of Etruscan art*. The orientalization in Etruscan art, especially the near-eastern influence, is claimed to be a result of their contact with the Greeks and Phoenicians, but I suspect the opposite. Given that the Etruscans were called Pelasgians (according to Myrsilius of Lesbos), and the Pelasgians ruled the Mediterranean 232 years prior to the Phoenicians according to Nelme, as well as the Etruscan alphabets being various forms of the Pelasgian one, it appears the Etruscans are the driving force of this cultural diffusion. Their alienness to the rest of the world implies they were a much older culture, or remnants of an ancient one, which civilized those referred to as Phoenicians, Carthaginians, Greeks, Romans and the like. The cultures with access to the Mediterranean, including the ancient Egyptians, might be a product of the Etruscans. Regardless, the Etruscans are not descendants of any known people, despite contrary claims made by oriental foreigners. Etruscan art, which incorporates elements of Near Eastern art, transformed these influences according to their un-classical, un-Greek, and surreal forms, what Grant called eerie and sometimes grisly. Etruscan architecture was un-Greek. Their way of life, their medicine and music, their personal appearance, the role of women being much freer, and the lack of social hierarchy differentiating them from the Greeks and Romans, most notably the absence of disparity between nobles and serfs, demonstrates they were older and unlike the despots from the east.

The greatest difference between the Etruscans and the so-called Romans and Greeks is their language. However, I suspect much of the Latin we're familiar with is a creation of the Middle Ages and that characteristic makes it similar to Greek and other Indo-European languages. The ancient Latin is descended from Etruscan. No less than half of Italy spoke non-Indo-European languages. Rome was quasi-Etruscan. It is an act of violence towards common sense to suppose Romans and Etruscans shared a city without speaking the same languages, especially since the kings of Rome were claimed to be Etruscan. Furthermore, the very families that made Rome an empire were of Etruscan origin and Celtic in appearance. How is it possible that the alleged Italic language of Rome survived but the Etruscan languages did not, yet Etruscan is considered Old Italic? This reminds me of the difference between English and Auld Ænglisc (Old English), a progression of improvement, cultural diffusion, and in some cases, corruption. There is no indication that the Latins exterminated the majority of the ancient Italian cultures.

Northern Italy, known to the Romans as Cisalpine Gaul (Gaul this side of the Alps), had an extensive Etruscan presence. Etruscan artifacts are found all over France, even in Northern France, as well as Southern Russia. I don't think the current narrative proposed by historians is correct because the very alphabets and customs of the so-called Germanic and Celtic people are traceable to Etruscan origin. I suspect the majority of Greek and Roman history is unknown because so much of it was reintroduced to Europe in the Middle Ages rather than being a continual succession of accounts, and this history may be no better than a compilation of forgeries and guesswork. The gaps in chronology may be the result of burning libraries in Alexandria, Constantinople, and various kingdoms in Europe.

It is curious how the Near East philosophy of the Greeks was introduced to Europe by the very people who destroyed so many of its writings. Thomas Astle wrote (Orig. Prog. Writ. p. xii.), "The Arabians or Saracens, whose wild and barbarous enthusiasm had destroyed the Alexandrian library in the seventh century, were the first people who were captivated with the learning and arts of Greece; the Arabian writers translated into their own language many Greek authors, and from them, the first rays of science and philosophy began to enlighten the western hemisphere, and in time, dispelled the thick cloud of ignorance, which for some ages had eclipsed literature."

Apparently the Caliph Almanzur's grandson Almamun obtained copies of the best books from the Greek Emperors, which were translated by the Arabian literati. Astle continued (Ib. p. xiii), "It will hereafter appear, that it was from the Arabians that these western parts became first acquainted with the Greek philosophy; and from them, several branches of science were introduced into Europe as early as the ninth century, and even into Britain before the end of the eleventh, in which, and in the three succeeding centuries, several Englishmen travelled into Arabia and Spain, in search of knowledge; amongst others, Adelard, a Monk of Bath; Robert, a Monk of Reading; Retinensis, Shelly, Morley, and others, of whom mention is made in the seventh chapters."

Again (Ib. p. xvi), "The taking of Constantinople, by the Turks, in the beginning of the fifteenth century, was an event which contributed to the general restoration of learning; at that time many learned Greeks fled for protection into Italy and Germany, where they were kindly received, and where they diffused science with great success.

"The chair of St. Peter was in the 15th and 16th centuries filled by several Pontiffs, who successively protected learning and learned men. Nicholas V. Pius II. Leo X. Clement VII. and Sixtus V. will be remembered with gratitude by posterity, for the patronage they afforded to literature.

"The first of these, may be considered as the founder of the Vatican library at Rome; the others were considerable benefactors to it, and by their industry and influence, greatly enriched that inestimable repository; and many of the succeeding Pontiffs, have with great success, followed their example.

"The Vatican library is divided into **three parts**. The first is public, and every one has access to it at different hours upon certain days; the second is kept with more privacy; and **the third is only to be seen by persons of certain distinctions**, or by those who have express permission for that purpose: this is called **the sanctuary of the Vatican**."

These details, among many others, lead me to conclude that the majority of European history is a product of the late Middle Ages, after the invention of the printing press. Pliny the Elder and others mention Demaratus, a rich merchant who, with his craftsmen, is claimed to be responsible for the Hellenization of Etruscan art and society c. 657 BC. But Dionysius of Halicarnassus (3.46.3-5), who is the most detailed source on Demaratus, doesn't account for what he did after settling at Tarquinii, other than building a house, marrying a local noblewoman, and having two sons, Arruns and Lucumo. He wrote, "There was a certain Corinthian, Demaratus by name, of the family of the Bacchiadae, who, having chosen to engage in commerce, sailed to Italy in a ship of his own with his own cargo;

and having sold the cargo in the Tyrrhenian cities, which were at the time the most flourishing in all Italy, and gained great profit thereby, he no longer desired to put into any other ports, but continued to ply the same sea, carrying a Greek cargo to the Tyrrhenians and a Tyrrhenian cargo to Greece, by which means he became possessed of great wealth. But when Corinth fell a prey to sedition and the tyranny of Cypselus was rising in revolt against the Bacchiadae, Demaratus thought it was not safe for him to live under a tyranny with his great riches, particularly as he was of the oligarchic family; and accordingly, getting together all of his substance that he could, he sailed away from Corinth. And having from his continual intercourse with the Tyrrhenians many good friends among them, particularly at Tarquinii, which was a large and flourishing city at that time, he built a house there and married a woman of illustrious birth. By her he had two sons, to whom he gave Tyrrhenian names, calling one Arruns and the other Lucumo; and having instructed them in both the Greek and Tyrrhenian learning, he married them, when they were grown, to two women of the most distinguished families.

"Not long afterward the elder of his sons died without acknowledged issue, and a few days later Demaratus himself died of grief, leaving his surviving son Lucumo heir to his entire fortune. Lucumo, having thus inherited the great wealth of his father, had aspired to public life and a part in the administration of the commonwealth and to be one of its foremost citizens. But being repulsed on every side by the native-born citizens and excluded, not only from the first, but even from the middle rank, he resented his disfranchisement. And hearing that the Romans gladly received all strangers and made them citizens, he resolved to get together all his riches and remove thither, taking with him his wife and such of his friends and household as wished to go along; and those who were eager to depart with him were many. When they were come to the hill called Janiculum, from which Rome is first discerned by those who come from Tyrrhenia, an eagle, descending on a sudden, snatched his cap from his head and flew up again with it, and rising in a circular flight, hid himself in the depths of the circumambient air, then of a sudden replaced the cap on his head, fitting it on as it had been before. This prodigy appearing wonderful and extraordinary to them all, the wife of Lucumo, Tanaquil by name, who had a good understanding, through her ancestors, of the Tyrrhenians' augural science, took him aside from the others and, embracing him, filled him with great hopes of rising from his private station to the royal power. She advised him, however, to consider by what means he might render himself worthy to receive the sovereignty by the free choice of the Romans."

Notice how Dionysius of Halicarnassus never mentioned what kind of "cargo" Demaratus traded. The lack of specificity is concerning, as is the detail of an eagle snatching his hat, disappearing, and then returning it. I live in a region with eagles; they don't behave that way. Even more problematic is that historians rely on Pliny the Elder's account (*NH* 35.43.152) that the art of pottery making was transmitted to Italy, but he didn't exist till the first century AD. How would he be a reliable source regarding the diffusion of pottery five to seven centuries prior? The archeological dating of the distribution of Protocorinthian ovoid aryballoi in Etruria, South Italy, Sicily, and elsewhere, which would've been one of the things Demaratus acquired wealth from, ***does not correspond to the the "historical" demise of the Bacchiad regime*** that Demaratus fled from. (Mur. Etr. p. 10.)

Pliny named the potters: ***Eucheir*** (Good Hand), ***Diopus*** (Work of God), and ***Eugrammus*** (Good Writing). These are ideas contained in the ***Maker***, God, who makes things, hence is a craftsman. ***It reeks of the triune nature of the sun***. We see this with ***Brahm*** (Brahma, Vishnu, Shiva), ***Saturn*** (Pluto, Neptune, Jupiter), ***Kronos*** (Hades, Poseidon, Zeus), ***Noah*** (Ham, Japheth, Shem), etc.

No one should suppose that writers could create accurate accounts of history five to seven centuries prior without archeological evidence to support them, yet, in regards to these artifacts that were buried in tombs, not discovered till the Renaissance and much later, the findings just happen to match what historians claim, yet it reads like astrotheology. Were Pliny and Dionysius grave robbers? Did they unearth all the pottery objects, write history based on them, and then bury them again? How did these writers come up with their accounts? How is "archaeological evidence" corroborating what those writers had no way of knowing save for repeating earlier accounts that no longer exist? It seems something else is going on. How can anyone be certain that the story of Demaratus isn't an allegory to describe the mercantile and pottery traditions? Perhaps we'll never know because archaeologists and scholars couldn't allow their findings to create the narrative, but rather they used those old accounts to explain their findings.

The claims made by Herodotus, of the Etruscans being from Lydia, were based on fictitious etymological analogies. Archaeological evidence demonstrates that the cultural links between the Etruscans and Lydians is sparse. Etruscan art and customs, as well as mythology and alphabets, are akin to Phoenician, and have much more affinity with Syrians than with Lydians and other zones of internal Asia Minor. Dionysius of Halicarnassus debunked Herodotus by acknowledging that the Etruscan laws, religious customs, and other institutions were entirely different than those of Lydia. (Grant, Ib. p. 239.) My only contention is that the presumption of this system and art coming from Phoenicia and Syria is based Mosaic history, which I've demonstrated in *Spirit Whirled* is untrue. I suggest, even though I could be wrong, that this system of religion, culture, and empire is coming from Etruria, and the Phoenicians were indigenous to Italy, not Syria or Lebanon. The Etruscan and Roman languages are Celtic, not from the Orient. The affinity is a result of their setting up commercial locations all over the known world, not the result of oriental conquest or migration en masse.

There is no evidence, in the archaeological record, of cultural breaks in the life of Etruria. This debunks the proposal of large-scale migration occurring in the later portion of the 2nd millennium BC or in the earlier portion of the 1st millennium BC. Grant also highlighted that the logistics of movement and settlement en masse were beyond the power of peoples at those times. (Ib.) The name

Etruscans is a Latin placeholder term. Each Etruscan city-state was culturally different, especially if the Italians of old were similar to the modern Italians in the sense that they don't think of themselves as Italian, but rather Roman, Venetian, Sicilian, Sardinian, Napolitano, etc. We in America generalize our ancestors as European, but the cultures there are different and the people think of themselves as different, even though they descend from similar ancient stocks. Etruscan city-states were individualistic in terms of their physicality, their customs, and art. But much of the tombs look like burial places for wealthy foreigners. There are not sufficient inscriptions from the era to decipher the language or describe what their culture was like. The Etruscan temples look like the precursor to what Greeks used, not the successor of that style.

Many of the Etruscan gravestones have waves surrounding them, a pattern that is used by navigators. Bologna is not far from Venice. If Betham is correct, that the first great colony of the Phoenicians was Italy despite Carthage and Tyre, it may account for the close relationship that the Caeritans had with the Carthaginians, who allegedly allied to fight against the Phocaean Greeks, which resulted in the retaking of Corsica by the Etruscans after the battle of Alalia c. 540-535 BC. It was a tactical victory for the Greeks, but they paid such a devastating price that it was a strategic victory for the Etrusco-Phoenicians. Given that Punic is Sicilian Phoenician, the language spoken by the Carthaginians, it might indicate that the Sicilians are descended from the Caeritans. Remember, some of the locations scholars identify in the physical world are not proven, beyond doubt, to be the actual locations written about. Much of it is guess work, albeit based on artifacts and such. It's not known who controlled Telamon (Talamone), though Grant suspected it was the Rusellans (from Rusellae, now Roselle). The fact that basic details, about some of the most strategic and significant locations of the Etruscan Empire, are unknown demonstrates how little certainty there is about Italian history.

Another detail that supports the indigenous nature of the Etruscans would be the akroteria at Poggio Civitate, and the terracotta roofing, along with the abundance of ridge decoration during this early phase of Etruscan architectural terracottas. *They were were alien to the Greek world* according to Rystedt. (Acquarossa IV (1983) pp. 159-63.) Rystedt was of the opinion that the Etruscan roofing has so much in common with the elaborate wooden superstructures of Villanovan huts that *nothing less than a direct continuity of indigenous tradition can be involved*. (Ib. p. 161.) The complexes at Acquarossa and Poggio Civitate, though they share features, are technically and stylistically different. (Rystedt, Ib. p. 145.) Scholars can't prove the chronology of this. They can only guess. They suspect it was c. 625-580 BC. *There is no evidence to prove they were the first of their kind built in Etruria*. Not only that, *there is no evidence to prove that this type of roofing and construction was brought to Etruria by Demaratus and his fictores* only *one generation before the date* commonly attributed to the appropriate phase at the two sites. (Mur. Etr. p. 7.)

It's claimed that Syrian craftsmen, not Greek ones, introduced monumental stone sculpture in Caere and Bononia. Here we have another possible Phoenician characteristic. How does anyone know the technique is not something Etruscans learned abroad and brought back? How do we know the technique is not something Etruscans invented? Deriving history from archaeology relies on subjective pattern recognition rather than actual accounts surviving the times. It isn't even known how the "Syrian" sculptors arrived.

The Etruscologists, whose work compiled *Murlo and the Etruscans* (p. 8.), submitted that some of the aristocratic Etruscans were covering their roofs with terracotta before the alleged arrival of Demaratus. It's claimed the Euboeans brought a variety of Greeks into a long-standing network of East-West commerce that had revolved around a Cypro-Levantine-Sardinian axis since the Middle Bronze Age around 770 and 700 BC. (Mur. Etr. p. 9.) The status quo claims that the Mediterranean was under the dominion of the Minoans, but their tablets use mostly Etrusco-Phoenician letters. Scholars like Bishop Thirwall and William Betham claimed that it was the Phoenicians who civilized the Greeks, that when they first encountered them, the Greeks hadn't even learned how to harness fire yet. The peopling of Crete would require shipbuilding and navigation skills, something that a Greek population would not be capable of if they were primitive. The use of letters was given to the Greeks by the Phoenicians circa 750-500 BC. So how could Minoans be using them circa 1500 BC? I suspect this is the farrago, the covering up of the ancient universal maritime empire whose epicenter was exactly where one could expect it to be: Italy and her neighbors.

It's more likely that the Phoenicians civilized the Greeks and helped them learn shipbuilding and navigation, enabling them to people Crete. The Minoan craftsmanship is not as good as the Egyptian, but the Minoans appear Egyptian, which might support the claims that Athens was an Egyptian or Etruscan colony. I suspect that the chronological adjustment needed to rectify history is for the Phoenicians to be recognized as Etruscans (ancient Italians), who were Celtae (European), not people from Asia Minor, and they were indigenous to Italy.

14 VILLANOVA, POMPEII, & EUROPEAN LANGUAGES

According to W. L. Brown (*The Etruscan Lion* (Oxford 1960), 27-45.), cited by Nancy Winter (Mur. Etr. p. 81.), the depictions of Etruscan lions are similar to the Phoenician models, indicating the Etruscans learned their technique from the Phoenicians. But I suspect this is resolved by recognizing the Phoenicians came from Etruria. The Villanovan culture is claimed to be the earliest phase of the Etruscans. It seems the Phoenician palmettes are connected to leonine heads. Others have observed this possibility, but I have not seen anyone else use the universal system of priestcraft to demonstrate it. It's hard to tell whether the lion replaced the palmette in an official capacity (regarding the priesthood), or if the Etruscans did it out of taste, preferring the more impactful lion's head, or gorgon's face, to the palmette. But the feline, lion, palmette, lotus, and lily symbolism was used to signify the sun, life, god, wisdom, and the like. The royalty of Europe either adopted this symbolism by using the fleur-de-lis, or it proves an unbroken descent from the ancient ruling classes that originally used this symbolism.

Which nation is known for the use of the fleur-de-lis? France, who is also known for her sun-king. This symbolism was used by the Dominican Order, which was founded in France at the beginning of the 13th century. France was partially Etruscanized; Etruscan objects were found from the Bouches du Rhône region all the way up to Haute-Marne (Northeast France). The Phoenician word for *lion* is *lis*, the French word for *lotus, or lily*. The Phoenician city *Lixus*, or *Lisus*, is named after the area's abundance of lions. In this case, the *X* functions as an *S/Z*, as in *Xavier* or *Xaca*. The mosaics at the site have the Thalassocratic symbol of Pontus, a clear mark of the sea people.

Which came first? Was it the Egyptians using the Indian lotus and the lion as representatives of the sun, or the Etrusco-Phoenicians using the palmette and the lion as representatives of the sun? The latter would've been transmitted to Egypt through the Phoenician use of Egyptian Thebes (Luxor) as a capital. Did this symbolism originate in India and work its way through the rest of the world? How could that occur without maritime capabilities, especially since Brahmins weren't allowed to travel beyond the region of modern Pakistan? Did it all originate in Egypt and make its way to India and Europe through the Phoenician mariners? Are my inquiries ill formed? They could be. I am merely one man asking questions based on available research, but there is so much unpublished information that it's akin to making sense of a puzzle in which half of the pieces aren't available.

Rystedt noticed a parallel of the absence of horses in the form of protomes (used to decorate Greek sculptures, architecture, and pottery) and on bronze cauldrons. The horse is painted on revetment plaques and tiles at Acquarossa. The jewelry from the Barberini and Bernardini tombs, in Palestrina, Lazio, about 28 miles southeast of Rome, displays the most complex examples of feline iconography from Etruria. (Rystedt, Mur. Etr. pp. 83, 84.)

Jocelyn Penny Small studied Etruscan Banquets and concluded that the Etruscans do not slavishly follow Greek models. (Mur. Etr. p. 87.) She placed a strong emphasis on the fact that **the Etruscans are not Greeks**. The Etruscans, though lovers of wine, women, and song, similar to the Greeks, valued and pursued these customs in ways that were much different from the Greeks at times, as well as enjoyed them in ways similar to the Greeks at other times.

The etymology of the name **Pompeii** is uncertain. Its spelling conforms to a Latinized version of Etruscan cities, a pattern that scholars have not yet determined the reason for, which is the plurality of the name, seen in cities like **Veii, Tarquinii, Volsinii, Vulci, Falerii, Podium Bonitii**, etc. Latin names for Etruscan towns also terminate in **-ae**, another form of plurality, seen in **Volaterrae, Ripa Arranciae, Careiae, Figulinae, Fregenae, Orclae, Pistoriae,**

Rusellae, and *Faesulae.* It is equivalent to calling these locations by the people's names, i.e., the Veians, the Tarquinians, Volsinians, Vulcians, etc., or in other words, it'd be like calling America *Americans.*

The Sarnus River (Sarno) granted sea-people easy access to Pompeii. The root of this word is *Sar, rock*, and *lord*, also seen in *Tyr, Tur, Tsar, Sur, Sir*, and *Tyre.* Pompeii was an important site going back to the Etrusco-Phoenician maritime empire, a critical location that a region can't afford to lose without suffering substantial economic decline and social strife. The statue of an Etruscan in Roman clothing, dated to the 1st century BC, demonstrates that the Etruscan language was used at least till the time of Julius Caesar, whose last name is Etruscan. According to Dr. Jeffrey A. Becker, the lower hem of the short toga carries an Etruscan inscription: *"auleśi meteliś ve[luś] vesial clenśi / cen flereś tece sanśl tenine / tu θineś χisvlicś"* which can be interpreted as, "To (or from) Auli Meteli, the son of Vel and Vesi, Tenine (?) set up this statue as a votive offering to Sans, by deliberation of the people." (*TLE* 651; *CIE* 4196.)

The Eruption of Mount Vesuvius destroyed Pompeii, along with Herculaneum and many villas surrounding the area, allegedly in 79 AD. Archaeology revealed that it was a multi-cultural epicenter, which would've made it crucial to the Roman Empire. The ***building of Eumachia***, the ***largest building near the forum of Pompeii***, is commonly broken down into three parts, the chalcidicum, the porticus, and the crypta. ***The purpose of the building is unknown*** *to modern historians*. The symbolism around her looks similar to other Magna Mater (Great Mother) symbolism.

While I don't accept Moses or Cadmus are historical figures, Astle cited an author (see his Enquiries concerning the first inhabitants, language, &c. of Europe, p. 104-109) on page 30 (Orig. Prog. Writ.), "Mr. Wise insists, that Moses and Cadmus *could not learn the alphabet in Egypt*; and, that *the Egyptians had no alphabet in their time*. He adduces several reasons to prove that they had no alphabet till they received what is called *the Coptic*, which was introduced either in the time of the Ptolemys, or earlier, under Psammitichus or Amasis; and these letters, which are *the oldest alphabetic characters of the Egyptians that can now be produced, are plainly derived from the Greek*. It seems to us, that if the Egyptians used letters before the time mentioned by Mr. Wise, *they were probably the characters of their neighbours the Phœnicians*."

Phoenicians were distinguished by the epithet of Tyrian or Sidonian, but also Pelasgian, which Dionysius of Halicarnassus wrote was also the name by which Tyrrhenians (Etruscans) were called. Though Sidon and Tyre were principal cities in Phoenicia, the navigators made Egyptian Thebes their capital (Luxor) during the time they possessed the empire of Asia according to the Greek General Conon. The history of Egypt, which was never named Egypt, is taught from a Common Era Abrahamic perspective. The whole Jewish history is mythology. The first mention of Moses by a Greek writer isn't until c. 273 AD. Historians accepted the accounts of Josephus that the Egyptians were ignorant of arithmetic and astronomy before being instructed by Abraham, which no serious researcher can accept. According to Abrahamics, all mankind lived together in Chaldea till the days of Peleg. (Univ. Hist. Vol. IV. p. 332, 375; Sir Isaac Newton's Chronology of Ancient Kingdoms, London, 1728, 4to.) This was debunked by language, phenotypes, and archaeology.

Astle wrote (Orig. Prog. Writ.), *"The characters and alphabets of all the countries east of Persia, have no connection with, or relation to, the Phenician or its derivatives, except only where the conquests of the Mahommedans have introduced the use of the Arabic letters.* The Shanscrit characters are the prototype of the letters used in India; namely, of the *sacred characters* of *Thibet*, the *Cashmirian*, *Bengalese*, *Malabaric* and *Tamoul*; the *Singalese*, the *Siamese*, the *Maharattan*, the *Concanee*, &c. The Tangutic or Tartar characters, and the Shanscrit, seem to have proceeded from the same source, as they are similar in their great outlines; but *whether the former is derived from the latter, or the latter from the former, is not easy to determine."*

Again on p. 49, "There are several alphabets used in different parts of Asia, which are entirely different not only from the Shanscrit, and all those proceeding from that source, but also from Phenician, and all its derivatives."

The characters and alphabets may not be connected, but the sharing of words between the Celtic, Roman, and Sanskrit led scholars to believe in diffusion from the Orient, which I suspect is inverted. Col. Wilford recognized that the Sanskrit alphabet, when stripped of double letters, and the ones unique to it, has the same sixteen letters as the Celto-Etruscan system (Asiat. Res. Vol. X. p. 152.), *"The Sanscrit alphabet, after striking off the double letters, and such as are used to express sounds peculiar to that language, has a surprising affinity with the old alphabets used in Europe, and they seem to have been originally the same."*

Lemuel Dole Nelme published *An Essay towards an Investigation of the Origin and Elements of Language and Letters*, in which he wrote (p. 78), "The Pelasgic symbols (or letters) were only 13 in number, and are said to have been received by the Etruscans, or rather retained by them; for *that people appear to have been of Pelasgic extract*: their symbols are delineated in our plate, and the powers of them are perfectly reconcilable to the powers of our radicals."

A 13-letter Phoenician-Pelasgic alphabet indicates it is based on an earlier Etruscan alphabet consisting of only twelve letters. Gorius and Swinton recorded the 12-letter Etruscan alphabets. By correcting the record of the Pelasgians being Italians (Etruscans), then the source of all the alphabets of Europe becomes Italy, which is my claim based on this information. Tamil, a language that allegedly descended from one that no longer exists, had 16 letters originally. The oldest inscription in India only dates to the 3rd century BC. There are much older inscriptions in Italy. Therefore, the affinity between Celtic, Roman, and Sanskrit is the result of Italian expansion. Italy is situated in between both cultures, but the ancient Italians are Celtic, not Oriental.

If I take Astle's writing and substitute the word *Pelasgi* with *Etruscan*, an obvious picture emerges. "These Phoenicians were called *Etruscans*, from their passing by sea, and wandering from one country to another. We learn from Herodotus, that the *Etruscans* were descendants of the Phenician Cabiri, and that the Samothracians received and practiced the Cabiric mysteries from the *Etruscans*, who, in ancient times, inhabited Samothrace. The *Etruscans* settled colonies in several islands of the Ægean Sea; as Samothrace, Lemnos, Thessaly, all the old Hellas, Argolis, Arcadia, and also the sea coast of the Peloponnese."

Though the Illyrian (Slavic; Slavonic), Russian, and Bulgarian alphabets are derived from the Greek, there is an Etruscan influence as well. The symbol that was ascribed to the Phoenician and Etruscan *M* was assigned to the Coptic *S*, and this change also occurred in the Cyrillic. While it's claimed that the Armenian letters are the descendants of the Greek ones, they differ from them. The only Armenian letters that resemble the Greek ones are the *phi* and the *omicron*. It appears that Armenian has Chaldean or Hebrew influence.

From the Roman alphabet we get the Lombardic, the Visigothic, the Saxon, the Gaulish, the Franco-Gallic or Merovingian, the German, the Caroline, the Capetian, and the Modern Gothic. The Lombardic and Caroline writing (Capetian on account of it being restored by Hugh Capet c. 987 AD) both degenerated into Modern Gothic, which isn't Gothic at all because it had nothing to do with the Goths or Visigoths in Italy and Spain. Like the Cathedrals, it was called "gothic" on account of it being of poor taste and barbarous. It was barbarous on account of its great variety and numerous abbreviations that made it difficult to read, much like modern day text messages.

If the Pelasgians were Etruscan, who are the Phoenicians, and polygonal masonry is Pelasgian, which is Etruscan (Italian), and if the polygonal masonry in Peru is an example of cultural diffusion, who is the only culture capable of transmitting it?

15 AMBER & NORDIC EXPANSION

According to Annette Rathje *Banquet and Ideology* (Mur. Etr. p. 96.), *we have to reconsider the role of the Phoenicians as agents in the cross-cultural connections* between Greece, Etruria, and the Orient. She was a proponent of *the active role of the Phoenicians in transmitting Oriental luxury items to Etruria* and that *they were active in the transmission of ideas that led to the incorporation of eastern customs in Etruscan society*.

I suggest the identity of the Phoenicians needs to be reconsidered. The language of the Celts, Romans, and Indians has undeniable affinity. The mythology of the Etruscans, when not shared with the Greeks, corresponds to the Phoenician mythology. Researchers succeeded in recognizing the affinity between cultures all over the world, but few have explained the origin of this system. The culture responsible for this system wasn't adequately identified until now. Even as late as the 18th century, the origin of letters and writing was still uncertain, and while many scholars refrain from making claims, they seem to agree that the most likely candidate was the Phoenicians.

Much of the Italic material, though large and extensive, is still unpublished, or it is not well-published. (P. Gregory Warden, Mur. Etr. p. 137.) Amber was popular for luxury objects in the 7th and 6th centuries BC, especially in Southern Etruria, Latium, Umbria, and Picenum. *The source of this amber is still unknown because the amber has not been properly analyzed.* Sicilian amber, and other Mediterranean amber, or Simetite, has no succinic acid but high sulfur content. Baltic amber normally has a higher content of succinic acid. The translucent reddish color of the Etruscan amber indicates Baltic amber, but until it is properly tested, no one will know. Judging by appearance, most of the amber found in Italy during the Iron Age looks like it is from the Baltic. This is significant because of what Polybius wrote, that *everything north of the region stretching from Tanais* (north of the Black Sea) *to Narbo* (Narbonne, France), *was unknown.* Polybius wrote in a time when only members of the priesthood and those connected to them were literate. If it can be depended on, it indicates the Nordic lands were unknown in the 2nd century BC. Yet the Iron Age is from c. 1200-550 BC. Some of the Etruscan amber pieces date to the Iron Age, c. 6th-7th centuries BC. *How can the amber being used by Etruscans trace to Nordic provenance if those lands were unknown?* I suggest that those lands, should the amber be of Nordic provenance, were explored by Etruscans, and that the Nordic people are a diaspora from the ancient Italians just like the ancient Britons were. Should both claims be true, that the lands were unknown yet the amber used was from them, then it indicates that this is the period in which they were being explored and colonized, and while not known in a broad sense, pioneers were already mining rare commodities, such as amber, and keeping their locations secret to preserve exclusivity and rarity, much like the Phoenicians did with Britain and its abundance of tin. What could motivate people to risk their lives exploring Northern Europe? According to Pliny (Natural History, 37.12), amber figurines could sell at a higher price than a slave, "So highly valued is this as an object of luxury, that *a very diminutive human effigy, made of amber, has been known to sell at a higher price than living men even, in stout and vigorous health.*"

It isn't common to see people on Etruscan tomb paintings wearing amulets, and the amber figurines look like fertility amulets or something of the sort. Warden conceded that *even though the Etruscan ambers seem Oriental, it is difficult to cite exact parallels in Near Eastern art.* (Mur. Etr. pp. 139-140.) What if Near Eastern art is merely a European take on their encounters with Oriental culture and their fascination with them?

The Etruscan depictions of cats generally don't correspond to the Attic depictions. According to Neil B. Todd (Cats and Commerce, Scientific American 237, 5 (Nov. 1977) 103.), cats take up residence on ships and come and go at will, so the seas become their highways whereas they are barriers for most animals. Ashmead, another scholar, wondered if cheetahs lived in Etruria or if their depictions were a figment of the Etruscan artists' imaginations. If they're not a figment of imagination, perhaps extra focus on cats will lead to important discoveries regarding cultural diffusion.

According to Astle, the boustrophedon mode of writing, which is of very high antiquity, was designed after the way an ox plows, which goes backwards and forwards from right to left and then left to right. He wrote (Orig. Prog. Writ.), "***The oldest Greek letters***, which are written from right to left, ***are nearly Pelasgic***, as appears by comparing the first Greek alphabet in plate I, with the Pelasgic alphabet in the same plate.

"The Latin alphabet is said to have originally consisted of sixteen letters. ***The G at first was supplied by*** C, which stands in its place, and K was continued in an old Roman alphabet; ***but after G was added, C was generally used for it, and then K was thought a superfluous letter***. The letters F and H, are frequently excluded [in] the Latin alphabet. The Latin, in ancient times, had no sound for the V, but that of a vowel: they supplied the Greek *Y* (upsilon) by their V, when they wrote Greek words in Latin characters.

"The consonant V, was the Æolic Digamma, and answered in power to the Phenician Vau, and the Latin F. The Latins used the F, to express the sound of the V consonant, as ***Fotum, Firgo***, for ***Votum, Virgo***; but when they used V for a consonant as well as a vowel, it afterwards became an F, or the P aspirated, answering to the

Greek Φ (ph). The Greeks rendered the V consonant, by the diphthong *ov* (ou).

"The Q was reckoned a double letter CV, and was anciently pronounced like C; the Sabines and Etrurians never used it, says Mr. Jackson, (vol. iii, p. 177); but is was an ancient Latin letter, and, though not in the primitive Latin alphabet, yet it is in the Arcadian."

The letter Q has been added to the Phoenician alphabet under the guise of Qoph, but it doesn't exist in the primitive versions of Etruscan or Phoenician. If scholars cannot concede Qoph didn't exist in the Phoenician, then it is a sign of forgery to include it in ancient alphabets, or, it is a sign that Phoenician is younger than Etruscan, because it didn't exist in Etruscan. The *Kilamuwa Stele,* which wasn't discovered till an expedition by the German Oriental Society that occurred between 1888 and 1902 AD, is claimed to be Phoenician from the 9th century BC. The craftsmanship is much better than matching alphabets from half a millennium later. The letter qoph is used. Therefore I suspect it is forgery.

The entire history of Europe is predicated on astrotheology, yet even by Nelme's admission, ***the Pelasgians were a maritime people 232 years before the Phoenicians acquired a maritime power in the Mediterranean sea***. This would make the Etruscans older than the Phoenicians, which would be why there is not enough literature remaining from the ancient Italians to decipher their languages, and why that which remains doesn't correspond to Indo-European, even though Rome was quasi-Etruscan. Nelme wrote (Ib. p. 81), "—some of their descendants improved upon the novelty, by exchanging the name of **Pelasgians** for that of **Etrurians**, for which they were detested by the Scythians, etc."

He continued (pp. 81, 82.), "Their detection operated in the declension of their civil power, and the loss of their language: thereto the Roman succeeded, which was a mixture of various dialects, all derived from the Pelasgic, but corrupted by the Oscans, Sabines, Samnites, and other nations (all Italian); which in process of time became blended with the Greek, another branch of the Pelasgic, or Etruscan tongue, of which *Linus* is called the *refiner,* and is also said to have written the exploits of Bacchus (Noah) in *Pelasgic* letters, about 1067 years after the deluge, and 1281 years before Christ. Orpheus, Pronapides, (Homer's master) and Thymætes, did the same."

My analysis and conclusions are not that controversial. I acknowledge much of what the status quo discovered about the structure of language, mapping it out, and the interchanging of letters. The primary difference between our conclusions is that I am not content with the cause of the system being Jehovah. The systems of language and alphabets are the results of priestcraft: mortals, not gods.

16 IRISH & PUNIC-MALTESE

The affinity of the Celtic, Roman, and Sanskrit languages has been demonstrated, yet the Brahmins were not allowed to travel past the borders of modern-day Pakistan into the region of modern-day Iran. The Indians are not known for being a maritime nation. Neither are the Chinese. Asiatic races did not have the physical prowess to defeat and subjugate European cultures en masse, nor did they possess weaponry to give them an advantage in combat. The opposite was true. Italians had the mining resources, strategic locations for supply chains and fortifications, and other logistical infrastructure to maintain an empire, even prior to being imperialistic. European farmers defeated the Ottoman Empire at the Battle of Vienna. The spread of this system from the east, through military campaigns, is not possible. The languages and archaeological record of ancient Italy demonstrate that no Asiatic culture made an impression on Europe en masse.

The Chinese, though they had lodestones and seafaring boats, hadn't discovered the art of navigation all the way into the 19th century. The cultural diffusion found throughout the world cannot be a result of the Celestial Empire of China. Gutzlaff observed this from 1831-33 AD (Voy. China. p. 87.), "The whole coast of China is very well known to the Chinese themselves. As *their navigation is only coasting*, they discover, at a great distance, promontories and islands, and are seldom wrong in their conjectures. They have a directory, which, being the result of centuries of experience is pretty correct in pointing out the shoals, the entrances of harbours, rocks, &c. As *they keep no dead reckoning, nor take observations*, they judge of the distance they have made by the promontories they have passed. They reckon by divisions, ten of which are about equal to a degree. *Their compass differs materially from that of Europeans*."

The cultural diffusion in locations that possess the mythology, language, and architecture *of the ancient Italians* requires a maritime empire to transmit it during a time when only a few cultures were capable of seafare. There is only one in the archaeological record so far: the Etrusco-Phoenicians. Though the term "Semitic", as applied to languages, wasn't introduced till the end of the 18th or early 19th century by Eichhorn and admitted to be eminently calculated to mislead by Archbishop Trench, it was applied to Phoenician and suggested that Ancient Hebrew is only a shade removed from

Phoenician. William Betham, who, after debunking the claim of Hebrew's affinity with Phoenician and establishing the Celto-Etruscan's affinity with Phoenician, claimed the *Celto-Etruscan is the true key, every division of which fits the words, and opens the long hidden treasure to our view*. (Etr. Celt. p. 10.)

According to Etruscologists Jocelyn Penny Small (Mur. Etr. p. 89.) and Michael Grant (The Etr. p. xviii.), when scholars remove their Greek sunglasses, they will see the Etruscans through modern eyes and behold that *they are not Greeks* and are regarded as a nonclassical, *native strain from Italy*. Either the ancient maritime empire originated in Britain or it originated in Italy and spread to Britain when the Etrusco-Phoenicians peopled those islands. I propose that the difficulty in figuring out Italy's history is the unwillingness to conceive that the Phoenicians are ancient Italians, indigenous to Italy, not to Asia Minor as religious narratives suggest. *Dionysius of Halicarnassus lists Saturnia* (Italy) *as one of the towns first occupied by the Pelasgians and then by the Etruscan civilization.* According to Betham (Ib.), *"The Pelasgoi were but Phœnician mariners*, who were to be found, not only in Greece, but every where a ship could approach the coasts of the Mediterranean."

But how did the symbolism for Egypt get to the Americas? According to Herodotus (4:42), the Phoenicians were employed by at least one Egyptian king (Necos) to sail around Africa, an account that even he didn't believe at the time, so it is likely that their employment took them all over the world during various stages of their empire, and much of it was kept secret, just like the British Isles, which were peopled by Phoenicians so long ago that no one can accurately date it. But the languages and alphabets used by the Britons, along with the artifacts and religious customs, demonstrate Etrusco-Phoenician ancestry.

The affinity to the Plumed Serpent's symbolism ascribed to sun gods like **Kukulkan** (Mexico), **Waji** (Egypt), and **Wadjet** (Egypt) might be dated to c. 3100 BC if the Egyptian dates are accurate, but I don't think they are for reasons explained in *Spirit Whirled*. However, even if the dating of **Waji**, **Wadjet**, and **Kukulkan** (Quetzalcoatl) is prior to the 14th century, then the ***plumed serpent signifying the sun is the greatest example of cultural diffusion in the ancient world***, which would indicate Egyptians arrived in America, or Americans arrived in Egypt, long before people reached the "New World" in 1492 AD. If this is not the case, then the ***plumed serpent in both cultures is the greatest archeological forgery***, and that evidence must be used to convict and condemn whatever institutions created these archetypes in Egypt, Mexico, or perhaps both if the symbolism is forgery in both locations. ***There is no in-between.*** The situation is the same regarding the Tuscaloosa Indian artifact known as the *Rattlesnake Disk*, which uses a Sicilian Phoenician version of the hamsa symbol and is allegedly dated to 1300 AD. It is either an example of specific cultural diffusion prior to Spaniards reaching the "New World", or it is archaeological forgery.

Vallancey wrote (Ant. Ir. Lang. p. 19.), "If an affinity of the Irish language with the Punic be allowed, this discovery will throw great lights on the darker periods of the Heathen Irish history. It will show, that though the details be fabulous, the foundation is laid in Truth. It will demonstrate the early use of letters in this island, because nothing but *that use* could preserve the least affinity from the flourishing era of Carthage to the present, a space of more than 2300 years. It will account for the Irish assuming to themselves the names of **Feni** or **Fenicians**, which **they have retained through all ages**. It will with the same certainty account for their giving the name of **Bearla Feni** (the Phœnician tongue) to one of their native dialects. In fine, it will show, that when they adopted the Phœnician Syntax, they confined their language to oriental orthography, while it harmonized itself out of its primitive consonantal Celtic harshness, by the suppression of many radical letters in the pronunciation of words."

Again (Ib. p. 22.), "The Irish historians do all agree, that **they received their letters from the Phœnicians**, and that their language was called **bearla Féne** or the **Fenician dialect**, of which their ancient manuscripts bear sufficient testimony."

This was an appeal to authority and consensus. I couldn't care less about what Irish historians think or what they agree on. I care about what can be demonstrated. But there is more than language to corroborate these ideas. Vallancey and other historians of the time thought Britain was already peopled prior to the Phoenician arrival, yet no one noticed the likelihood of the Phoenicians being Etruscans as far as I can tell. Although Betham suggested the possibility of the Etruscan navigators being referred to as Puni, and claimed Italy was the first great colony of the Phoenicians, his work maintained that the Phoenicians originated in the Near East. Vallancey and other scholars called the Irish people who dwelt in Britain prior to the arrival of the Carthaginian "pirates" by the name **Nemedians**. Vallancey claimed they were Fomorians, or African pirates, in Ireland at several periods: that they introduced the art of building with stone and lime, astronomy, &c. that they adored certain stars, supposed to have power from the God of the Sea, either to guide or mislead the ships: that at length they overran the country, and made a complete conquest, drove out the **Nemedians**, and laid the island under tribute. (Ib.) The Fomorians are a product of Irish mythology and their story looks like astrotheology. However, Vallancey thought they allegorized the Carthaginians. It may be an instance where the details are legendary but the general idea is based on people from the ancient past.

Carthaginians spoke Punic, which is specified as Sicilian Phoenician, and with the Phoenician portion of Sicily being in the southern Tyrrhenian Sea, the Carthaginians and Irish are likely descended from Etruscan stock. Sicily is unique in its location because it's where the Tyrrhenian, Ionian, and Mediterranean seas merge. Greeks and mariners from Asia Minor and North Africa have no need to go out of their way to reach Sicily en route to Carthage because they used **Malta** instead, hence the Phoenician name of Malta signifying *place of refuge or sanctuary*. During these times, North Africa was Celtic (Etrusco-Phoenician), which you can see in their ancient cities like Lixus. The Berbers of North Africa spoke

Punic. Their real appellation was **Numidian**, which is philologically **Nemedian**. Even if the Fomorians were an allegory for Carthaginian or some other Phoenician stock of pirates, the Nemedians who were driven out of Ireland might have been ancient Numidians. Much of the conflict during these ages might've been akin to powerful families within the same empire fighting with each other over valuable territory.

Vallancey wrote (Ib. pp. 22, 23.), "Orosius and even some modern authors, have gone so far as to deny the use of letters to the Carthaginians, before the Romans conquered that republic; and, as a proof of this, they quote many inscriptions in Roman characters from various places in Africa.

"It is true, **the Carthaginians adopted the Roman letter in the first Punic war**, which character it is very probable they brought with them to Ireland, as **no inscription has been found in this island in the Phœnician letter.**"

Name one culture that adopted the writing, language, or alphabet of the nation they were at war with prior to being conquered. Vallancey's claim seems invalid, but I could be wrong. Also, the fact that not one Irish or British inscription was found in their language using Phoenician letters is of great concern. The earliest Irish manuscripts are written in Latin letters, and everything regarding alphabets and language in Britain's historical record is admittedly deformed Roman and originally Italian in its structure.

Again from Vallancey (Ib. p. 23), "Of the Roman Saxon capital letters, the Irish use but three, all the others bear a very great resemblance to the primitive Hebrew and Phœnician, as given us by Scaliger and Postellus; and in the Chaldaic characters given us by the latter, are to be found, all those used by the ancient Irish, bearing the same figure and power."

The Phoenicians' first settlement in Spain was claimed to be **Cadiz**, or **Gadiz**, which Vallancey claimed was due to the friendly reception they received from the inhabitants, thus it was named after friendship. (Ib. p. 25) I don't know where he learned this, but the Irish word **cadas** is indicative of this concept. It appears he recognized forgery in Polybius's writing. He wrote (Ib.), "Polybius informs us, that the Carthaginians were the first foreign nation the Romans entered into an alliance with, out of their own continent; that a treaty of commerce and navigation was confirmed between them as early as the consulship of Brutus, which treaty was engraved on a marble pillar; and that this inscription was discovered so soon after as the second Punic war, when not a Roman was to be found who could read it. *Such an alteration had the Latin tongue suffered in so short a space!*" (Note the sarcasm.)

People make claims that Arabic is the oldest alphabet and Latin is some sort of reverse or inverted version of Arabic. Vallancey addressed it (Ib. pp. 25, 26.), "Nor can I agree with the whims and fancies of some learned men, that it was the vulgar Arabic spoken in Africa at this day.

"For it is well known **the Pœni** (Phoenicians) **were of another offspring and not of Arabian race**, and that **it is not yet 1000 years, since that tongue was brought by the Arabians into**

Africa.

"And as certain also it is, that the remnants of the Africans' progeny, as Leo Africanus hath recorded, have a different language from the Arabic."

G. Pietro Francesco Agius de Solandis wrote a treaty in the 18th century that preserved the remains of the Punic-Maltese and is also an Italian-Punic-Maltese dictionary. (*della Lingua Punica presentemente usata da Maltesi*, etc.) The following examples are drawn from Col. Vallancey's work comparing the Punic-Maltese to the Irish, and will be represented by PM (indicating Punic-Maltese) and Ir. (indicating Irish) so that you can see the affinity. Some of these may not look like they have affinity unless the reader is familiar with how Celtic transliterations use Latin letters to signify sounds that the letters are not associated with. For example, the combination of *bh* makes the sound of *v consonant*, i.e., *dubh* is pronounced like *dove*. The combination *dh* makes the sound of *g* or *y* depending on where it is placed in the word and what vowel follows it; if it's at the end of the word, it is silent. The value of the Irish-Punic affinity is so important that it ought to have been placed at the beginning of this book, but due to its technical nature, I placed it near the end so it wouldn't overwhelm casual readers. This original language undergoes subsequent changes in Armoric, Cornish, Welsh, and perhaps Manx.

(PM) *Samem*, the Heavens, (Ir.) *Samh*, the Sun, *samhra*, summer; (PM) *sema*, an assembly, (Ir.) *samhadh*, a congregation; (PM) *Baal, Belus*, and *Bel*, old names for the sun, (Ir.) *Bel, Bal, Beal*, the chief Deity of the ancient Irish; (PM) *Allai bier eq*, God bless you, (Ir.) *Iall beira dhuit*, may you repent. God forgive you; (PM) *iva b'alla*, a curse, (Ir.) *Jobhadh* (pronounced iva) *bio Alla*, may death come from the Almighty; (PM) *tummin*, truly, (Ir.) *tam ann*, that's true, truly; (PM) *ara!* interjection, (Ir.) *arah!* an interjection; (PM) *ardu*, the end or summit, (Ir.) *arda*, high, haughty, *ard*, a hill; (PM) *artap*, liquido, molle, vizzo, soft, flabby, (Ir.) *anairt*, soft—*tap* is an affix of the Arabic, signifying the overflowing of a river, hence *artap* may imply ooze, slab, mire—from *tap*, the Irish *tapbior, topar, tobar*, a well or spring; (PM) *baghda*, hatred, strife, (Ir.) *bagh*, a contest, a fight; (PM) *ballut*, an acorn, also a burying place, a monument, (Ir.) *bal-lacht*, the wall of a grave, a monument; (PM) *bandia*, a cord, a swing, a measure, (Ir.) *bann*, suspension, *bandla* and *bandal*, a certain measure used in the south, somewhat more than half a yard, by which coarse linens are sold in the markets under the name of bandal cloth, *bannlamh*, a bandle, a cubit in measurement; (PM) *ban-gham-mi*, the son of my uncle, (Ir.) *ban* is a son, as in the compound, *banscoth*, a son-in-law, *banta*, a niece (this is connected to the Hebrew word for son: *bn*, pronounced *ben*); (PM) *ghamt*, an aunt, (Ir.) *gean*, a woman, *ingean*, a daughter; (PM) *berqarqara*, or *casall bercarcara*, in Malta il più vicino Città Valetto, i.e. *bel* antica; *berquara* Augusta, grande, i.e., antico Augusto Villagio di Malta, (Ir.) *barrachas*, august, great power— overplus, *bar-cathar*, (cahar) an august city; (PM) *bin* or *ben*, a son, (Ir.) *ban* or *bar*, as *banscoth*, a son-in-law (that root of *bn* is also found in the Arabic word for son); (PM) *beni tè mutha*, figlio de la morte (son of death), (Ir.) *mughaim*, to be put to death, *teadh*, to grieve, *bani teadh mugha* (I think this would translate as grieving a dead son or a son who was put to death, but it might've just been Vallancey stringing the words together so the reader could see the similarity); (PM) *bir*, a well, a foundtain, (Ir.) *bior*, *bir*, a fountain, a well; (PM) *bua*, or *bva*, to drink, (Ir.) *buadh*, food, *ibba*, to drink; (PM) *beniet*, young woman, (Ir.) *benne-ette*, woman's age; (PM) *abu!* voce ammirativà! (admirable voice), (Ir.) *abo!* the war cry of the ancient Irish—now a common interjection of admiration; (PM) *challa*, or *challi*, to forsake, to abandon, (Ir.) *caillidh*, to lose, to destroy; (PM) *chall*, sharp, (Ir.) *calg*, a prick, a sting; (PM) *chafir*, to pardon, (Ir.) *cabhar*, help, assistance, relief, *for*, protection, defence; (PM) *ciacir*, meandring, scattering, (Ir.) *cearacadh*, wandering, straying; (PM) *da fra*, tresses, or locks of hair, (Ir.) *fraigh*, a bush of hair; (PM) *daqqa*, an act or deed, (Ir.) *deacdah*, a law; (PM) *dar*, a house, and improperly written (says our author) *dars*; (Ir.) *dars*, a habitation: *dae*, a house; *riogh-dhae*, a palace; (PM) *dar el binat*, a nunnery, a house for young women, (Ir.) *dae*, or *daras na bene*, a nunnery (see the word *ben*, O'Brien's dictionary); (PM) *dar*, *dir*, desire will, (Ir.) *deoir*, will, pleasure, *deoir*, *dior*, a proper inclination; (PM) *ghogiol* (armentum) a heard of cattle, (Ir.) *giogail*, to follow close, to herd; (PM) *fart*, an ox, bull, or cow, (Ir.) *fearb*, an ox, or cow; *mart*, the same; *og-wart*, an heifer; (PM) *fahhal*, a spiteful expression, also derision, (Ir.) *fala*, spite, malice; (PM) *fahhal*, a stall fed ox. Thus we call a libertine *fahhal*, and to a harlot, we commonly cry, *baqra* or *baqar*. (Ir.) *fail*, a stye, a stall; as *fail muice*, a pig-stye, *baccaire* and *boccar* are terms of reproach in Irish, fully answering the idea of the Punic word (this is laid up in the Latin *vacca*, cow, which is *bacca* with the interchange, giving another layer of symbolism to *Bacchus*); (PM) *barra*, besides, out of, (Ir.) *barr*, over and above, besides, the end; (PM) *basc*, below, at the bottom, (Ir.) *bas*, the base or bottom (I wonder if this signification is attached to the name of the *Basque* people); (PM) *bahu*, to empty, to make void, (Ir.) *bathamb* (pronounced bahu), to cancel, to blot out; (PM) *bedui*, a countryman, (Ir.) *bodach*, a rustic clown, old man; (PM) *beit*, a house, (Ir.) *bath*, *boith*, a cottage, hut, or booth (this is from Hebrew or Arabic, unless it turns out those languages took it from the Punic); (PM) *bet-al*, domus Dei (house of God), (Ir.) *both-all*, domus Dei (I wonder if this is the origin of the word bottle, or if brothel mocks a house of God); (PM) *bet e lem*, domus panis (house of bread), (Ir.) *both-lan*, domus satietis (house of satiety); (PM) *dem*, blood, kindred, (Ir.) *daimb*, kindred, consanguinity; (PM) *dor's*, fruit, (Ir.) *toradh*, fruit; (PM) *feithh*, to open, to discover, (Ir.) *feithea*, to overlook, to give attention; (PM) *emma*, but, (Ir.) *amh*, but, even, also; (PM) *engkarra*, imposition, (Ir.) *aincheard*, an imposter, *aincheara*, imposition; (PM) *esma*, hear me, hearken, (Ib.) *eisd me*, hear me, listen to me, more properly *eisd liom*; (PM) *far*, over, beyond, to transport from place to place, (Ir.) *for*, over, beyond; *foraimh*, a journey; (PM) *farac*, mirth, consolation; (Ir.) *forc, forca*, advice, consolation, *foch*, entertainment, hospitality; (PM) *fieg-ku*, powerful, puissant; (Ir.) *feadhmach*, potent, powerful, *feadh-cuaith*, an extensive country, (dominions); (PM) *fuq*, the summit, high above, (Ir.) *fa-uachdar*, upon the summit; (PM) *gha-dira*, standing water, marshy ground, slush, (Ir.) *go* or *ga*, the sea; *ga-direm*, water without passage; (PM) *ghain*, the face, front, the eyes, (Ir.) *cainsi*, the face or countenance (at the time these languages would've been diffused, the letter G didn't exist and the function was served by C); (PM) *ghana*, to sing, *canadh*, (pronounced *gana*) to sing; *do ghan sè*, he sings; (PM) *aghniq*, rich, prosperous, (Ir.) *aghmhárach*, fortunate, prosperous; (PM) *gh-arma*, a plenty of cord, (Ir.) *armhar*, or *arbhar*, corn, *aga-armhar*, plenty of corn; (PM) *gha-qal*, sensible, reasonable, (Ir.) *go-céill*, sensible, reasonable; (PM) *gha-aqqa*, a term used to mortify a strumpet. I believe (says our author) from *acca*, a famous harlot in our history; (Ir.) *giabhair*, a harlot, a strumpet, (Ir.) *aga*, addition, an augmentative, *giabhair-aga*, a very whore; (PM) *ghaz-el*, distinction, comprehension; (Ir.) *ceasa, geasa*, to see plainly and distinctly; the Arabic affix *el*, answers to the Irish prefix *con*, *as ad con-ceas*, I distinguished, or saw plainly; (PM) *gheaq*, tyhoides coccineus tuberosus, sea blubber, sea spunge, (Ir.) *gearg*, a blubber botch, or bile, any tubulous body, (PM) *ghuscia*, a place in Malta, but properly a sorcerer, a conjurer, (Ir.) *gu-sighe*; *gu* a lie—*sighe* a demon, a familiar spirit; *geasa*, sorcery; (PM) *gibu*, to give, to present, (Ir.) *geibhadh*, to obtain, to get; (PM) *hhabba*, corn, (Ir.) *arbhar*, corn; (PM) *hhadár*, to assist at a wedding, (Ir.)

adharadh, to join together; (PM) *hhai*, to live, (Ir.) *beatha*, to live; (PM) *hh-alleitu*, released, abandoned, (Ir.) *dealuighthe*, released, divorced, separated; (PM) *hhami*, hot, (Ir.) *tíme*, heat; (PM) *hham-ria*, reddish earth, also *hham-ria*, an ass, I believe (says our author) from his dun colour, (Ir.) *úim*, earth, *ria*, sky coloured, *ruadh*, red, *úim-rua*, red earth, *aimhréidhe*, obstinancy, strife (Vallancey thought this word seems more analogous to the qualities of this beast); (PM) *hh-apas*, a prison for slaves, (Ir.) *adhbhas*, a garrison, *abas*, a great man's house, *adhbha*, a dungeon; (PM) *haqem*, a man in power, a captain, (Ir.) *acmhuin*, potent, able, *airgim*, to plunder or spoil; (PM) *haten*, knowledge; (Ir.) *aitne*, knowledge, *aithni*, to know; (PM) *hazer*, an entrance, or forecourt to a palace, (Ir.) *asaidh*, to rest, or stop; (PM) *hhabar*, news, novelty, (Ir.) *abra*, a speech, *abar*, speak thou, *abrann*, bad news (*Abran* is also the month of April); (PM) *hhaniena*, pity, (Ir.) *anaoidhin*, pity, compassion, *is anaoidhin dhuit*, woe unto thee; (PM) *iassu*, old age, (Ir.) *aoise*, old age; (PM) *ieqerdu*, ruin, destruction, (Ir.) *eag-orda*, ruinous fragments; (PM) *ias-cesc*, shriveled with age, (Ir.) *aois-caiseac*, wrinkled with age; (PM) *i-dein*, the hand, the fist, (Ir.) *dorn*, the fist; (PM) *itqatta*, twisted, (Ir.) *athcasda*, returned, retwisted (you'll have to take into account the transliteration when you search for some of these on your own, i.e., this word will look like *atcasda* in Irish); (PM) *kadin*, a prolongation of time, (Ir.) *cáirde*, delay (this word also signifies respite and friendship in Irish); *do chur se air cairde*, he prolonged the time; (PM) *kafar*, to bind to a performance, (Ir.)

caithfidh, must, ought, (oportet) an impersonal compulsive verb; *comh-farran*, to keep by compulsion; (PM) *ghana*, to sing, (Ir.) *canadh*, to sing; (PM) *kàrès*, cruel, merciless, (Ir.) *cruas*, hardness, rigor; (PM) *kasma*, a gap, a chink, a separation, (Ir.) *casnadh*, split wood, chips; (PM) *ksim*, to divide, to bend, (Ir.) *casm*, to wind, to turn, to bend; (PM) *ka-vi*, strong, valiant, robust, (Ir.) *cath-fhir*, warriors; (PM) *k-scuir*, to separate the hull from the grain—chaff, also bran. (Ir.) *caith*, chaff; *scaradh*, separation; (PM) *laill*, the night, (Ir.) *daille*, the night; (PM) *tugurio*, casa rustica, a vile, a wretched hut, a cabin, (Ir.) *teagh*, a house, *uir*, mold, clay, *teagh-uire*, a house of clay; (PM) *mirgiarr*, or *megiarr*, two places in Malta, so called because near the sea shore, (Ir.) *muir-gearr*, close to the sea; (PM) *mieta*, a certain tax on any vendible commodity. The word is totally Punic, and has been used time immemorial by the Punic people of Sicily, Malta, and Gozo, (Ir.) *measta*, taxed. It is used in that sense in all the old Irish law books, and in the New Testament, Luke 11:1, *an domhan vile do* *mheas*; (PM) *mur-amma*, a country edifice, (Ir.) *múr-amagh*, a building or dwelling in the plains or country; (PM) *sena* and *snin* (a Phoenician word), the seasons, a year, (Ir.) *sion*, the weather, the seasons, *soinine*, the seasons; (PM) *sama*, heavens (called so in Punic), (Ir.) *samh*, the sun; (PM) *sebm*, a portion, a share, (Ir.) *seimh*, a small portion, single; (PM) *sciehh*, un uffizio decoroso, con cui si gloriano i literati, signiori, principi e governadori delle città (a decorous office, with which the literati, lords, princes and governors of the cities boast), (Ir.) *sgeith*, chosen, selected, *sci, scia*, to beautify, to adorn; (PM) *sara*, to combat, to fight, (Ir.) *saragha*, conquest, victory, *sarugha*, to overcome, to rescue; (PM) *sillura*, an eel, (Ir.) *siliou* (Armoricè; Armrocian) eels; *sahhta*, wasted, destroyed, (Ir.) *sachadh*, to sack, to destroy, *saghaidhthe*, destroyed; (PM) *lembi*, a vessel for working or stamping dough with the feet, (Ir.) *leim*, leaping, jumping, stamping; *bi, bia*, food; (PM) *levi* and *luvi*, to bend, or wring, (Ir.) *lubha*, to bend, or twist; (PM) *liti*, a grand procession, (Ir.) *lith*, solemn pomp, *laith*, a crowd; (PM) *loqma*, a bit of bread, a morsel, (Ir.) *loghda*, an allowance; (PM) *marbat*, (anello, a ring) Voce de Fenici, di cui il Salmasio, e Boccardo, parlano presso il Majo, da cui nacque marbut legato. Erbit, legare (to bind) *norbtu* ligamo, (Ir.) *mear*, a finger, and *beart*, an ornament or clothing; as *cois-bheart*, worn on the legs, i.e. stockings; *ceann-bheart*, worn on the head, i.e. a hat; these compounds are very common in the Irish; so *mear-bheart*, worn on the finger, i.e. a ring; (PM) *ma tra*, è difficile ritrovare un termine proprio ad esprimare questa voce, ma piuttosto per abbellimento di chi è dilletante della propria favella, ne altro significa, se non *sì è*, if so, say you so? (it is difficult to find a specific term to express this voice, but rather for the embellishment of those who are amateurs of their own speech, it does not mean anything else), (Ir.) *ma ta*, if so, *mar ata*, if so, *ma ta raidh*, if so said, *maturè*, soon, speedily, *ma-trath*, if in due time, *ma-atraidh*, if he said; (PM) *medd*, magnitude, prolongation, (Ir.) *meid*, bigness, magnitude; (PM) *meri*, to contradict, to thwart, (Ir.) *mearaigh*, to mistake, to err; (PM) *meut*, death, (Ir.) *meath*, decay, (death); (PM) *mut*, il Majo scrive muto, nomine conseravit mortuum, cum Phœnices mortem et Plutonem vocat (*il Majo scrive muto*, the name of the **dead man**, when he says **death** in Phoenician and and refers to **Pluto**; my translation might not be correct), (Ir.) *mudha*, dying, perishing, *meathadh*, to die, *mudha*, *mutha*, dying; (PM) *ml-alet*, a ball of wool, (Ir.) *mol-olla* (Munster dialect), combed wool, made up in a ball; (PM) *n'asciar*, to cut off, to exclude, (Ir.) *ascaradh*, separation, *eiscidh*, to lop off, to exclude, *eiscis agcionna dhiob*, their hands shall be cut off; (PM) *och*, a nun, (Ir.) *ogh*, a maid, a virgin; (PM) *ba schar*, good tidings, (Ir.) *ba-scéal*, good tidings, *sacarbhuig*, a confession; (PM) *casid*, *cased*, holy, undefiled, (Ir.) *cast*, undefiled, chaste; (PM) *q'al*, speech, (Ir.) *agall*, speech; (PM) *qala*, the breast, the bosom, (Ir.) *gaile*, the stomach; (PM) *qala*, the sail of a ship (This is the Carthaginian name of those ships moved by wind only, to distinguish them from ships of war, worked both by wind and oars), (Ir.) *gál*, a gale of wind; (PM) *qarab*, an approaching, (Ir.) *gara*, near, at hand, *gar-ab*, not close; (PM) *qatta*, a stick, club, or spear, called so in Phoenician, (Ir.) *gath*, a spear or javelin; (PM) *qaber* and *cabir*, a grandee, a nobleman, (Ir.) *cairbre*, the name of several Irish princes; so also **Charibert**, one of the Kings of France. **Cairbre** also signifies a territory; (PM) *q'elp*, hounds, (Ir.) *cu-ealb'a*, a pack of hounds, i.e., hounds in a hear, or drove; (PM) *q'uqqu*, eggs, (Ir.) *ugh*, an egg; *orca*, eggs; (PM) *ra*, sight, (Ir.) *abhra* (avra), *rombra*, *radharc*, sight; (PM) *rabba*, plenty, increase, (Ir.) *rabbac*, fruitful, plentiful; (PM) *r'as*, a headland, a promontory, (Ir.) *itros*, a headland, *ross* has the same meaning; (PM) *riebh*, wind, (Ir.) *aréabh*, wind; (PM) *r'aqba*, a cavalcade, (Ir.) This is a compound of the Irish *eac*, a horse, a word still used at Constantinople, *ar-eic*, upon horses; (PM) *sabaq*, strong, valiant, (Ir.) *sab* and *sabag*, able, strong; (PM) *sfaffaq*, observing, careful, frugal, (Ir.) *sabhallach* (sabalac), careful, sparing.

It's important to consider that the Punic-Maltese words were recorded a millennium after the Ottoman Empire invaded North Africa and Europe, so by that time there are, of course, Arabic and Hebrew words infused into the vocabulary. On this, Vallancey wrote (Ib. p. 44.), "It is evident, that in this catalogue of words given by Agius, as Punic, many are purely Arabic and some are Hebrew. The difference in orthography between these Maltese words and the Irish words corresponding thereto is easily accounted for; the Maltese use the Arabic character, and the difficulty the author found in transcribing them into the Roman letter, has already been shown in his own words. The author of this essay, has frequently conversed with the various nations of the Mediterranean Sea, particularly with the Africans, and from his own experience can testify that every nation of Europe, would differ in the orthography of the same word, particularly in the *guttural* and aspirated consonants; the Irish would be the most similar to the original African dialect. Quintilian observes, in his time they were much embarrassed how to transcribe the ancient Latin, having lost the power of several letters; and Claudius and Origen say the same."

17 ONE SOURCE

In Irish, *Mór* has a different meaning than in Welsh. It adheres to the Phoenician *maur* (great, lord, prince), whereas the Welsh adheres to the Latin *mare* (sea), yet with the interchangeability of *u, v,* and *w*, we see the Welsh pronunciation, *mawr*, is the Phoenician *maur*. Inis Mór is the largest of the Aran Islands off the west coast of Ireland, so, in this instance, *mór* pertains to the island's size, like we see in *Great* Britain. I suspect this difference is because the Welsh is descended from the ancient Irish or Wild Scots, and not the other way around, and it is evidence that the Irish language is much older on account of its affinity to Sicilian Phoenician (Punic). If the Irish language is not older than the Welsh one, then the maintaining of Phoenician meanings in Irish words indicates that the Irish experienced less cultural diffusion than the Welsh did.

Words get disguised to such a degree that they appear irreconcilable till traced through several languages on account of alterations (transposition, omission, addition, or change of other letters). There are many words in **Greek**, **Latin**, **Italian**, **Spanish**, **French**, **British**, **Irish**, and **Sclavonian** (Baltic region) that begin with **K**, **C**, or **Q**, or, as in the case with Teutonic, the letter **H**, that undergo this process, in addition to each language's terminations. (Lhuyd, Arch. Brit. p. 24.) Until this knowledge is acquired, philology is impossible to understand at a level that could be used to discover cultural diffusion, just like one can't read until he *learns* to read. There are no shortcuts. The work must be done. Lhuyd added (Ib.), "The Ancient Romans us'd not the Letter **G** at all; till added (as Plutarch informs us) by **Spurius Carvillus** (c. 230 BC). *'Et cùm C ac simpliciter T non valuerunt, in G ac D Molliuntur.* (And when C and simply T did not prevail, they softened in G and D.) Quint. L. I. C. XI. "Prævaluit postquam **gamma** vice functa prius **C**. Auson." (It prevailed after Gamma had worked twice before C. Ausones were a people in Etruria synonymous with Oscans.)

Again (Ib.), "When **C**, **K**, or **Q** is the **Initial** Letter in the **Ionic**, **Æolic**, **Latin**, **Teutonic** or **Irish**, those words frequently begin with **P** in other Dialects of the **Greek**, and in the **Welsh**, **Cornish** and **Armorique**; and the same Alteration, happens sometimes in the Middle and Final Syllables; whereof [we] see some Examples in the Changes of the Letter **P**.

"*Q* is so much the same, with *K* or *C* that it seems to have been absolutely superfluous amongst the *Romans*; and that the *Greeks* deservedly cashir'd it, retaining only its use as a numeral Note. In the *Armorique* it's a common Letter, but was never receiv'd (as far as I could hitherto observe from Old Manuscripts) into the *Welsh* and *Irish*; *Cu* or *Ku* rendering it useless: nor can we discover tho some Learned *Grammarians* have maintain'd the contrary, any more necessity of it, than the *Italians* and *Spaniards* have of inventing a new Letter instead of *G* in such words as *Guastare, Guado, Guera,* &c. And that 'twas redundant amongst the *Romans* is confirm'd by their doubting when to make use of it."

The original systems and religions are based on the most important system: Nature. But they've been dressed up in so many lies as to be unhelpful to those who aren't taught their origins and significations. While it brings no joy to address the history of the priest class, it is unavoidable because the very tool that separated the Pelasgians from anyone else was the use of letters, which is why they were called the *Dioi Pelasgoi*, or *Holy Sailors*. I suspect this is a Greek corruption because the *-oi* termination that signifies *plurality* in Greek is pronounced like the Latin *-i*, which also indicates plurality when it terminates a word. *Dioi* (*Διοι*), is a Greek version of *Dii*, meaning *Gods*, which would be the Latin plural form of *Deus*, meaning *God*. In fact, the *Dioi Pelasgoi* signify the *Wandering Gods*, or the *Gods Who Wander By Sea*, which could be an allegory for the *Wandering Luminaries* (planets) through the *Sea* *of Stars.*

I've already considered these possibilities, but it doesn't change anything because none of my work is staked on the title or name of the navigators from the universal maritime empire. Even if the stories around them are astrotheology dressed up as history, I can demonstrate that there was a universal system that originated in Italy and spread throughout the world, one that we still experience the effects of today. The Greeks do not use **Deus**. They use **Zeus** and **Theos**, which, after studying the changes and interchanges between letters in different cultures and dialects, you should be able to recognize as the same word. The corruption may be a result of interacting with Latin culture by the time the description for the Etruscans, the **Holy Sailors**, was given by Homer. Even during the chronology of Homer (8th century BC), there are examples of Greek that appear to be descended from Latin and not the other way around, contrary to what we've been taught. It may indicate that Homer's work is a modern forgery.

I've demonstrated that the likely origin of the Phoenicians is Sicily due to Punic being Sicilian Phoenician. But to get to Sicily and Carthage, and then to Cadiz, the Bay of Biscay, Armorica, Britain, and eventually the Netherlands, Denmark, Sweden, Norway, and the Baltic region, they had to learn the craft of seafare, and the empire that dominated the Mediterranean consisted of Etruscans, who the Greeks called **Tyrrhenians**, **Tyrsenians**, and **Pelasgians**.

This skill of seafaring, in my opinion, originates in Italy because the transition from living in dwellings carved out of stone to building megalithic superstructures is present in the archaeological record. There are over 100 articles on my Substack that show picture-evidence for those interested. There's no evidence of mass migration into Italy during to substantiate claims of Europeans coming from the Caucus Mountains or Africa. But I concede that those areas of the Mediterranean that include North Africa, Eastern Europe, and Asia Minor were inhabited, in ancient times, by the cultures we call European or Celtic. It's apparent, in the languages and systems of civilization, that the Central Europeans have their origins from an Etrusco-Phoenician empire that preceded the Roman one. Wherever they were before that, if not in Europe, is something hasn't emerged in the archaeological record yet, in terms of culture, language, religious symbolism, and the other staples of the universal system.

Lhuyd wrote (Ib. p. 34.), "We must therefore necessarily allow, that whatever Nations were of the Neighbourhood, and of one common Origin with the Greeks and Latins, when they began to Distinguish themselves for Politeness; must have preserved their Languages (which could differ from theirs, but in Dialects) much better than them. And consequently *[it is] no Absurdity to suppose a great many words of the Language spoken* by the Old *Aborigines*, the *Osci*, the *Læstrigones*; the *Ausonians, Oenotrians, Umbrians* and *Sabins*, out of which the *Latin* was composed, *to have been better preserved in the Celtic than in the Roman.*"

Why don't you look up where those cultures are from? Behold the indigenous Europeans. Georgii Stiernhielmii wrote (Præf. de Linguarum Origine, ad M. G. De la Gardie Ulphilam Redivivum.

Stock. Quarto. 1671.), *"The Etruscan, Phrygian, and Celtic languages are all related; derived from one source."*

Lhuyd continued (Ib. p. 35.), "And that being granted, it must also be allowed that the **Celtic** (as well as all other Languages) has been best Preserved by such of their Colonies as from the Situation of their Country, have been the least subject to Foreign Invasions; whence it proceeds, that we always find the Ancient Languages are best retained in Mountains and Islands.

"But as no Situation of a Country could fully secure its Language from Alteration, so we shall always find, that of the Radical words, some are better preserved in one Language, and some in another.

"Of Radical words those seem, Generally speaking, to be Ancienter that consist of fewest Letters: for when words agree only in Part, those that have the Additional Letters or Syllables are for the most part, (for it often happens otherwise) the Derivatives: And according to that Observation, we shall find, that a Great number of words in the **Latin** Tongue *might better be Derived from their Neighbouring Languages*, than those Languages from it."

Etruscan has fewer letters for the same words, indicating it is more ancient than Greek. Greek and Latin are both derived from Etruscan languages mixing with the oriental languages. But the Latin agrees more with the Etruscan because it is directly descended from it, which demonstrates Latin is older than Greek. Greek corresponds more with Hebrew than Latin does, and both Greek and Hebrew maintain a numerical value found ascribed to their letters, a tool so useful that no language borrowing from them would discard it, proving that Greek and Hebrew are both younger than Latin. *The Real Universal Empire* is from Italy. I am proud of this claim, for I am the only one who demonstrated it. In this regard, the Etruscan family I descend from is significant, given the lies that were spread about us and about ancient Italian history by culture vultures. Let my work put an end to theirs. I hope you enjoyed this book and thank you in advance for recommending it if you did.

For the glory of God,

Caesar.

ABOUT THE AUTHOR

For those interested in a more technical, archaeological, geographical, and philological analysis of this work, or who would like to stay up to date with my latest research, endeavors, and media appearances, subscribe to the Dylan Saccoccio Newsletter on Substack: greattide.substack.com.

<u>Other Titles</u>

Spirit Whirled

The Tale of Onora

Get Mad or Get Realistic